STREET SMARTS

STUDY GUIDE

USING QUESTIONS TO ANSWER CHRISTIANITY'S
TOUGHEST CHALLENGES

GREGORY KOUKL

ZONDERVAN REFLECTIVE

Street Smarts Study Guide
Copyright © 2023 by Gregory Koukl

Published in Grand Rapids, Michigan, by Zondervan. Zondervan is a registered trademark of The Zondervan Corporation, L.L.C., a wholly owned subsidiary of HarperCollins Christian Publishing, Inc.

Requests for information should be addressed to customercare@harpercollins.com.

Zondervan titles may be purchased in bulk for educational, business, fundraising, or sales promotional use. For information, please email SpecialMarkets@Zondervan.com.

ISBN 978-0-310-17826-2 (softcover)
ISBN 978-0-310-13917-1 (ebook)

Scripture quotations, unless otherwise indicated, are taken from the New American Standard Bible® (NASB®). Copyright © 1960, 1971, 1977, 1995 by The Lockman Foundation. Used by permission. All rights reserved. www.lockman.org.

Any internet addresses (websites, blogs, etc.) and telephone numbers in this book are offered as a resource. They are not intended in any way to be or imply an endorsement by Zondervan, nor does Zondervan vouch for the content of these sites and numbers for the life of this book.

All rights reserved. No part of this publication may be reproduced, stored in a retrieval system, or transmitted in any form or by any means—electronic, mechanical, photocopy, recording, or any other—except for brief quotations in printed reviews, without the prior permission of the publisher.

Published in association with the literary agency of Mark Sweeney & Associates.

Cover design and art: Brian Bobel

CONTENTS

Study Guide Instructions v

SESSION 1: Getting Ready for the Street. 1

SESSION 2: Questions Keep You Safe. 21

SESSION 3: Intel for Navigating the Street 43

SESSION 4: Atheism: The Best Explanation for the Way Things Are? . . 61

SESSION 5: Evil: Atheism's Fatal Flaw 87

SESSION 6: Jesus the Son, Christ the Savior 109

SESSION 7: The Bible: Ancient Words, Ever True? 133

SESSION 8: God: The Science Stopper? 153

SESSION 9: Abortion: Only One Question. 175

SESSION 10: Marriage, Sex, Gender, and Common Sense. 207

Epilogue 231

STUDY GUIDE INSTRUCTIONS

AN ADVENTURE IN LEARNING

You are about to embark on an exciting adventure in learning with one of the finest training tools available. This *Street Smarts Study Guide*, together with the accompanying *Street Smarts Video Study*, provides an easy-to-follow, well-reasoned plan for responding to opposition to your Christian convictions.

Some of the information here may be a bit challenging at first. Yet if you work through this material carefully and at your own pace, you'll not only become "conversationally competent" yourself; you'll also be able to teach others, as well.

In these ten sessions you will learn:

- The reason why "gardening" effectively is critical to a bountiful spiritual "harvest"
- Why using questions is the safest and most effective way to maneuver with others in challenging conversations on spiritual matters
- How to recognize the way the devil "schemes" to mislead people whom he has blinded to the truth
- Why relativism, the first heresy, informs almost every type of opposition you'll face on the street
- How to respond to a trio of distractions you'll encounter with your atheist friends
- Three powerful reasons why theism is the best explanation for the way things are
- Why the problem of evil is one of the best evidences *for* God and *against* atheism
- How the Trinity is a solution, not a problem
- Why Jesus is the only way of salvation

- Why God was the science starter, not a science stopper
- The single question that's key to resolving the abortion debate
- How to respond to concerns about slavery and "genocide" in the Old Testament
- How to maneuver safely through conversations on the thorny issues of marriage, sex, and gender
- How to address each of these issues using the questions and sample dialogues provided to help guide you through the minefields

Using This Study Guide

The *Street Smarts Study Guide* is meant to be easy to use. The material is presented in outline form so you can quickly see the relationships between the main ideas. You'll also notice that the text is punctuated by special sections, each with its own unique purpose.

Demonstrating Mastery

At the beginning of each new session, you will find a review of some of the "Self-Assessment" material from the preceding session. Be sure to do this exercise—either on your own or with someone else—before each session. It has two purposes. First, as you work to recall the main points of the prior session, the ideas will be reinforced in your mind. Second, as you review the past material, you'll be better prepared for the next session.

Ambassador Skills

The "Ambassador Skills" sidebars provide tips that will help you improve your interactive skills when engaging in conversations so you can present your ideas in a winsome and attractive way.

Reflect a Moment

The "Reflect a Moment" sections give you a chance to momentarily step aside from the main point and ponder a related idea. It may be an insight, a clever application, or a reflection designed to make the lesson more practical or meaningful.

Dialogues

The sample dialogues are important segments designed to take your training experience from the passive stage to the active stage. Using provocative opening questions, these model conversations show you how to put your new knowledge to work in productive ways with others.

Going Deeper: Information for Self-Study

In the "Going Deeper: Information for Self-Study" sections, you'll find suggestions for activities to do on your own. You'll put what you've learned into practice in meaningful ways. This step is vitally important for mastery learning.

Self-Assessment

Another critical element of mastery learning is recall, the ability to bring to mind the important details you've been taught. The self-assessment quizzes are a powerful tool to help fix the salient details of the course in your mind so you can recall them quickly when you need them.

Interactive Group Study Questions

The "Interactive Group Study Questions" are interactive exercises to stimulate discussion and reflection on the important ideas in each session. If you're going through this study on your own, you will sometimes need to enlist the help of others for these sections.

Food for Thought

Additional items under the heading "Food for Thought" are included at the end of each session to supplement your learning experience. They expand on concepts or principles dealt with during the sessions.

The Secret to Mastery Learning

Finally, one secret guarantees mastery of this material: *teach it to others.* Anyone who is a student of the material can become a teacher of the material. Perhaps you can give talks in your church, Sunday school, youth group, homeschool, or small group using the notes in your manual and adapting the material to your unique situation.

Whatever way you choose to pass the material on, the benefit will be twofold: you'll get a better grasp of the material by teaching it, and whoever you share it with will benefit, as well.

GETTING READY FOR THE STREET

I. A Confession

A. To be perfectly candid, evangelism is hard for me.
1. That probably surprises you, given my background. I've spent nearly half a century defending Christianity.
    a. Frequently one on one and many times before university audiences
    b. Sometimes on television and radio, often opposed by hostile witnesses
2. Even so, evangelism is a challenge. And I bet I'm not alone. Maybe you're like me.

B. Few things cause more guilt for believers than sharing their faith.
1. They feel guilty because they don't do it enough.
2. They don't do it because they're scared. And they're scared for good reason.
    a. Sharing the gospel and defending it—apologetics—often feels like navigating a minefield these days.
    b. For most of us, talking with others about Christianity doesn't come easily, especially when people are hostile.
3. It's one of the reasons we often stay off the "street," so to speak, when it comes to spiritual issues.
    a. We stay away from environments where we don't feel safe.

b. Most of us wouldn't wander into the local atheist club meeting or mingle with the marchers in a gay pride parade. It's too scary. We don't know how to handle ourselves.
 4. Guess what. The apostle Paul felt it, too. Listen to this:

 > And the Lord said to Paul in the night by a vision, "Do not be afraid any longer, but go on speaking and do not be silent; for I am with you, and no man will attack you in order to harm you, for I have many people in this city." (Acts 18:9–10)

 5. Jesus understood the risks, too.
  a. When he sent his disciples out on their first short-term mission trip, he told them, "Do not fear" three times in seven sentences (Matt. 10:26–31).
  b. Why? Because there were reasons to be fearful.
 6. Jesus said not to worry, though. They had an ally they could count on—the Holy Spirit.
  a. That's good advice, but it's often misunderstood because there's another detail a lot of people miss about the disciples' situation.
  b. Jesus didn't give this assurance at the beginning of his ministry, but in the middle of it.
 7. Here's what Jesus said at the beginning: "Follow Me, and I will make you fishers of men" (Matt. 4:19).
  a. Jesus was going to instruct his disciples and equip them.
  b. He was going to prepare them *before* they hit the street.

II. Prepping for "the Street"

A. That's the rationale behind *Street Smarts*.
 1. Following Jesus' example, I want to teach you how to be more effective "fishers of men."

2. I want to equip you to address the challenges to your Christian convictions you're going to face.

B. **Where is the "street"?**
   1. The "street" is anywhere you feel vulnerable, out of your element, or exposed to danger.
      a. We keep our distance from threats we don't think we can handle.
      b. Like the Hebrew spies encountering giants in the promised land, we feel like grasshoppers in *our own* sight. The challenges seem bigger than they are, and we seem smaller. The giants are real, but they're not as big as you think.

C. **I want you to consider something that intimidates lots of Christians, yet actually works in our favor.**
   1. There are many ways to show that Christianity is false. I'm sure that's something you didn't expect me to say, but it's true.
      a. Our story starts, "In the beginning God. . . ." If there is no God, though, then there is no story. End of issue.
      b. Christians are disciples of Jesus. If Jesus never existed, then our project never gets off the ground.
      c. If there is no soul that survives the death of our bodies, then when we die we stay in the ground. No one goes to heaven or hell, so what's the point of the good news?
      d. If moral relativism is true, and right and wrong are just a matter of personal opinion, there's no real sin—so judgment in a place like hell makes no sense anyway.
      e. Paul said that if Jesus didn't rise from the dead, people should feel sorry for us (1 Cor. 15:19).

D. **These challenges represent what might be called the "soft underbelly" of Christianity.**
   1. They are beliefs we hold that make us vulnerable because in principle they could be mistaken. Christianity, then, is falsifiable.

2. The possibility that Christianity can be disproved, though, is not a bad thing. It's a good thing.

   a. If a view is falsifiable (able to be shown to be false), then it is verifiable (able to be shown to be true).

   b. And that's exactly what Christians can do.

E. **Those challenges don't destroy Christianity because they don't succeed.**

   1. We have the evidence, and we have the answers—answers you will find in this course.

   2. In *Street Smarts* I will give you the tools you need to face and destroy the speculations raised up against the knowledge of God (2 Cor. 10:5). You don't need to be overwhelmed by the daunting challenges.

▶ Reflect a Moment

It's natural for us to feel vulnerable when we *are* vulnerable. Jesus anticipated this and warned us in advance. Paul experienced it and overcame it. You can overcome it, too, with a helping hand. Do you like taking tests? Most people don't. Do you mind taking tests *when you know the answers*? That's different. Here's the simple truth: the giants shrink when you learn how to deal with them. That takes information. It's part of the training Jesus gave his own team, and it's the kind of training you'll find here.

III. A Better Way: Get Street Smart

A. **Here's a quick summary of how *Street Smarts* works.**

   1. *Street Smarts* trades on a basic approach I explain in detail in *Tactics: A Game Plan for Discussing Your Christian Convictions*.[1]

---

[1]. See Gregory Koukl, *Tactics: A Game Plan for Discussing Your Christian Convictions*, 10th Anniversary Edition (Grand Rapids: Zondervan, 2019). In addition to providing a simple, three-step plan for effective interactions with others, *Tactics* also describes in detail how to graciously use a variety of maneuvers to help you discover the errors in your friends' thinking and to help them see their mistakes.

2. That plan is a powerful technique to keep you in the driver's seat of difficult conversations with skeptics and challengers—yet in a safe, genial, and amazingly effective way.

🟥 Reflect a Moment

The tactical approach has completely transformed my ability to make a difference for Christ. If you haven't done so already, reading *Tactics* will be a big help, although *Street Smarts* will still serve you well as a stand-alone guide to answering common challenges effectively, even if you're a newcomer to the tactical approach.

3. *Street Smarts* moves you beyond the basic game plan by expanding on the third part of that plan: using questions to expose a weakness or a flaw in another's mistaken views about God or God's world.
    a. In *Street Smarts* I focus on the larger issues themselves.
        (1) Atheism
        (2) The problem of evil
        (3) Abortion
        (4) Science and Christianity
        (5) Problems with the Bible
        (6) Marriage, sex, gender
    b. I'll give you the insight you need on how those challenges fail.
    c. I'll also give you the specific questions you need to point out those problems in a gracious way.

🟥 Reflect a Moment

The *Street Smarts* approach has proven itself over the decades I've been using it myself in countless hostile encounters. It has also been indispensable to thousands of others I've taught over the years, allowing them to maneuver almost effortlessly—and with complete safety—even in the most challenging conversations.

B. **The training consists of two parts.**
    1. First, the content

a. To use questions to answer challenges, you have to know the answers to the challenges.
   b. You have to see where the weaknesses are.
2. Second, the dialogues
   a. You need to know how to tactfully expose those weaknesses.
   b. You'll do that by using specific questions in a precise manner in conversation to be, as Jesus put it, shrewd but gentle.
3. So, for each challenge:
   a. I'll supply questions to help you smoothly enter the conversation.
   b. I'll then expand those initial questions into sample dialogues that will guide you forward according to the game plan, allowing you to bring those weaknesses to light in a gracious, disarming way.
4. These mini-dialogues will not be complete, of course.
   a. It's hard to know how any conversation will play out in the long run.
   b. The mini-dialogues will be enough, though, to get you going and move you in the right direction.
   c. Once you're in the driver's seat of the conversation—and that is a key advantage of the game plan—you'll gain momentum, making the rest of the dialogue much easier and more productive.

> **Ambassador Skills**
>
> Remember, these sample conversations are model exchanges. They're not precise scripts you have to memorize. Instead, you'll want to internalize the key questions and have a clear grasp of the basic direction you want to go. Take the core ideas I offer, then weave them into your conversations in a friendly way that fits your own personality.

5. I want to make a hard job easier for you.
   a. I'll give you both the content and the plan you need to move forward.
   b. By confronting the giants one by one, I'll shrink them down to size for you.

C. **A quick word of warning**
   1. The answers I'll give to the objections you'll face are good ones.
   2. The tactical game plan is solid, honed over thousands of hours of conversation with challengers and critics.
   3. Even so, there are no "silver bullets"—no guarantees.
      a. No good answer or clever technique will ensure anyone will turn to Christ. A host of factors shape a person's beliefs. Many have nothing to do with sound thinking.
      b. Emotions and prejudices, not just rational factors, play a huge part in forming a person's moral and spiritual opinion.
      c. Real conversions—as opposed to "decisions"—generally take honest soul searching, lots of time, and the powerful work of the Holy Spirit.

> **Ambassador Skills**
>
> Remember, evangelism is rarely tidy because life is not tidy. Do not despair if your conversations are messy and herky-jerky and initially seem to bear no fruit. The long-term impact of your faithful witness can be profound. Your task is to present the truth as clearly, as graciously, as persuasively, and as faithfully as you can. That's 100 percent your responsibility. All the rest is up to God—100 percent. You do the talking; God does the persuading.

Being effective on the street these days, however, means revising our thinking about evangelism.

IV. Changing Times

A. **Here's an admission that might shock you.**
   1. I haven't prayed with anyone to receive Christ in more than thirty years.

a. I've been a Christian nearly half a century, spoken on more than eighty university campuses, and publicly defended Christianity on six continents.

b. Yet I have not "led" anyone to Christ in decades.

2. I know that makes me sound like a loser. However, I've never been more effective for Christ than I have these last thirty years.

B. **From a biblical perspective, that makes perfect sense.**

1. I've stumbled upon an insight that could revolutionize your approach to evangelism.
2. I wish I'd seen it years ago since the Gospels and Acts are thick with it.
3. This biblical perspective can make your conversations easier, safer, and more effective than you ever thought possible.

First, the backstory . . .

C. **Simple times, simple gospel**

1. I came to Christ during the Jesus movement in the early 1970s. Back then we offered the simple gospel and invited people to receive Christ. Many responded.
2. Times have changed. The gospel is not "simple" anymore.
   a. The gospel is still the gospel, of course. The truth is still the truth and always will be.
   b. The way people *hear* the truth, though, has changed dramatically because the cultural conversation has changed dramatically.
3. In the '70s, people had a positive view of Christianity, and Christian words and concepts made sense to them. Now the culture is largely anti-Christian.
   a. The hostility is not just against the gospel proper but also against virtually every detail of the biblical view of reality:
      (1) What it means to be human
      (2) What it means to be gendered
      (3) What it means to be moral
      (4) Even what it means for something to be "true"
   b. Our task is to make the unchanging message—and its foundational ideas—more intelligible to contemporary ears.

🗨 Reflect a Moment

Lots of people think the smart crowd has weighed in and found Christianity wanting, both rationally and morally, so they have no reason to give our message a second thought. For many our words of hope are taken as words of veiled hostility, bigotry, and even hatred of outsiders.

   4. In short, the culture has moved on. Unfortunately, our methods have not.
      a. People don't understand our ideas, so they don't understand our message.
      b. The gospel seems obsolete, antiquated, and irrelevant.

That confusion can be spiritually lethal, as Jesus points out.

D. Roadkill
   1. In Matthew 13:18–23, Jesus tells the famous parable of the sower.
   2. Some seeds sown fall beside the road, and birds swoop down and carry them away. No mystery here. Hard ground, no growth. Some people just won't listen.
   3. But there's more to Jesus' point.
      a. "When anyone hears the word of the kingdom *and does not understand it*, the evil one comes and snatches away what has been sown in his heart" (v. 19, emphasis added).
         (1) The seed is sown "in his heart," yet something critical is missing.
         (2) The word sown in the hearer's heart is not understood.
      b. When people are spiritually puzzled, the word of life is quickly snatched away by the devil.
      c. By contrast, the "one on whom seed was sown on the good soil, this is the man who hears the word *and understands it*; who indeed bears fruit . . . some a hundredfold, some sixty, and some thirty" (v. 23, emphasis added).
   4. Here's the question: According to Jesus, what's the difference between the first person and the last person, between the one who bears nothing and the one who bears an abundance?
      a. The second person understands the message.
      b. The first person does not. He becomes roadkill.

> **Ambassador Skills**
>
> This insight is central to Paul's exhortation in Colossians 4:5–6: "Conduct yourselves with wisdom toward outsiders, making the most of the opportunity. Let your speech always be with grace, as though seasoned with salt, so you will know how you should respond to each person." The last phrase is key. If our evangelistic game plan focuses only on harvesting, then it's hard to tailor our communication uniquely *to each person*.

V. Spadework

A. **The insight: before there can be any harvest, there must be a season of gardening.**
   1. A good harvest is always dependent on sowing, watering, weeding, nurturing.
   2. When I was a student at UCLA in 1973, I was testing the Christian waters, asking questions, pushing back, and—eventually—listening.
   3. On Friday night September 28, 1973, I was ready.
      a. When the fruit was ripe, all it took was a bump for it to fall into the basket.
      b. When the spadework is done well, the harvest takes care of itself.
   4. Note, there are no altar calls or invitations to "receive Christ" in the Gospels or in Acts. That practice is historically recent.[2] So what was the early church doing? They were gardening.

B. **Two seasons, two workers, one team**
   1. Think about Jesus' words in John 4 after his conversation with the woman at the well.
   2. "'One sows and another reaps.' I sent you to reap that for which you have not labored; others have labored and you have entered into their labor" (vv. 37–38).

---

2. The "praying to receive Christ" practice is not part of the New Testament pattern. It entered the life of the church hundreds of years later. In Acts people simply preached persuasively, and listeners believed. The Holy Spirit brought conviction that led to humble faith. The closest thing to an altar call in the New Testament was a baptism, but that came after faith, not before it.

C. **Notice a critical calculus of evangelism according to Jesus.**
   1. One field—Sychar. Two different seasons—sowing and reaping, gardening and harvesting.
   2. One team—God's people. Two types of workers—those who sow and those who reap; those who garden and those who harvest.

D. **Go for the gold?**
   1. Some Christians are convinced we should try to get to the gospel in every encounter.
      a. Press for the decision.
      b. Close the deal.
   2. The impulse is right-hearted, but wrongheaded; this approach has problems.
      a. First problem: we're not listening to people long enough to learn their cultural language.
         (1) If we don't listen to understand *their* views, how can we communicate so they'll understand *ours*?
         (2) If our words of truth fall on deaf ears, there will be no understanding. Those precious gospel seeds get whisked away and the devil wins.
      b. Second problem: What about Christians who might be great gardeners but have only a harvesting model of evangelism?
         (1) The idea of pressing someone for a decision—especially in today's hostile environment—is simply too scary for them. They sit on the bench, out of play.
         (2) I'm completely sympathetic. Most of us are not good closers, so we never get into play. And when gardeners don't garden, the harvest suffers.

E. **Please do not misunderstand me.**
   1. Harvesting is critical. There'd be no kingdom growth without it.
   2. But without the spadework—the plowing, the planting, the cultivating—there's no kingdom growth, either.
   3. There is no good harvest without good gardening.

> **Ambassador Skills**
>
> I do not feel compelled to shoehorn the gospel into my conversations in an odd or artificial way, pushing toward the finish line when it's not natural for the circumstances. Even Jesus didn't get to the gospel in every conversation. In fact, his most famous moral discourse, the Sermon on the Mount (Matt. 5), was thick with bad news, not good.

No, I don't swing for the fences in my spiritual conversations with people. Instead, I have a different goal, a more modest one.

VI. Lowering the Bar, Raising the Impact

A. When I'm in a conversation that I hope will lead to spiritual matters, I never have it as an immediate goal to lead that person to Christ.
   1. I don't try to "close the deal." In fact, I don't have it as a goal to get to the gospel, though I may end up there.
      a. Do I want that person to come to Christ? Of course I do.
      b. Is the gospel necessary for that? Of course.
   2. Getting to the gospel is not the issue, though.
      a. According to the parable of the sower, the problem is the ground the seed falls on. There's no understanding.
      b. The hard ground needs tilling first before the seed can take root.

B. A more modest goal.
   1. Whenever I speak to a non-Christian audience, I always tell them that I'm not there to convert them. Instead, I tell them, "I just want to put a stone in your shoe." I just want to give them something to think about.
   2. I'm not in harvest mode. I'm gardening. It's the same way I do all of my witnessing, even one on one.

C. When do I get to the gospel?
1. I get to the gospel whenever I want.
   a. I get to the gospel when I think I can position it in a meaningful way that fits the natural flow of the conversation.
   b. I do not feel under obligation to force-fit the gospel into every encounter.
2. Jesus understood this.
   a. He took his time. He paced himself. He weighed his words to be sensitive to his audience and to the unique circumstances he faced.
   b. Often he went only halfway, giving the bad news. He got to the good news over time, but first he gardened.

Reflect a Moment

When I tell audiences the importance of gardening before harvesting, I can see in their eyes something slowly beginning to dawn on them. They're thinking, *I can do this.* Lowering the bar gets them off the bench and into the garden, and that means a bigger harvest in the long run.

VII. Who's in Your Garden?

A. **Years ago I realized I was not a harvester but a gardener. And I'm not alone.**
   1. Since the hard work is in the gardening, I think most Christians are gardeners.
   2. They just haven't thought of themselves that way since the option was never really open to them.

B. **Which brings me back to my original confession, the one that made me sound like a pathetic Christian, an evangelism loser.**
   1. You might have heard of the amazingly successful cold-case detective J. Warner Wallace.[3]

---

3. Wallace never lost a case that went to trial.

a. As an atheist, he applied his considerable skill as a detective to the Gospels and concluded from the evidence that Jesus rose from the dead.

   b. He became a follower of Christ, then an apologist, then a bestselling Christian author.[4]

2. Here's something you don't know about Jim Wallace.

   a. When he was an atheist, he was in my garden listening to the *Stand to Reason* radio show.

   b. I never led him to Christ, but my gardening in his life was critical to his conversion.[5]

3. Did you notice what happened? Somebody went into *my* garden and harvested *my* crop. Do I care? Of course not.

4. Remember Jesus' words "so that he who sows and he who reaps *may rejoice together*" (John 4:36, emphasis added).

   a. One field, one team

   b. Two different seasons, two different kinds of workers

   c. We all work together.

5. In the body of Christ, different people have different gifts.

   a. When it comes to working the field, some sow and some reap.

   b. That's what Jesus taught.

C. So how do you know if you're a gardener or a harvester? Here's how:

1. If what I've said so far *bothers* you—

   a. If you think I'm letting people off too easily

   b. If you think I should be pushing them harder to close the deal in spiritual conversations

   c. Then I suspect you're a harvester. And I'm glad you are. We need you.

2. If, on the other hand, what I've said *encourages* you—

   a. If you're thinking, *I can do this*, then you're probably a gardener.

   b. That would be most Christians, I expect, and we need you, too.

---

4. J. Warner Wallace authored books like *Cold-Case Christianity*, *God's Crime Scene*, *Forensic Faith*, and *Person of Interest*, among others.

5. Over the years, I have met many others who were "in my garden" as non-Christians who have gone on to accomplish significant things for the kingdom.

> **Ambassador Skills**
>
> If it's beginning to dawn on you that you might be a gardener like me, then make it your modest goal in conversations to put a stone in the other person's shoe. Focus your efforts on giving that person just one thing to think about. Don't worry about the endgame; just get busy doing some spadework.

   D. Remember, you don't have to swing for the fences.
   1. You don't even have to get on base, in my view. All you need to do is get into the batter's box—and that's what *Street Smarts* will help you do.
   2. Then let the Lord take things from there. That's the secret—and the beauty—of gardening.
   3. If you do that—if you get off the bench and get into play in simple ways that are friendly, yet moderately challenging, you're going to see a dramatic difference in your impact for the kingdom.
   4. Don't forget, the more gardeners there are, the bigger the harvest will be. Then "he who sows and he who reaps may rejoice together."

Once you're off the bench and out on the street, it really helps if you have a game plan. And that's what I'll give you in our next session of *Street Smarts*.

VIII. What Main Points Did We Cover in This Session?

   A. First, we candidly acknowledged that evangelism can be tough in today's culture.
   1. Sharing and defending the gospel often feels like navigating a minefield.
   2. Yet the first believers shared that same concern.
      a. Jesus warned his disciples there would be conflict ahead.
      b. Even the great apostle Paul sometimes struggled with fear of speaking up.

B. **Second, we learned that adequate knowledge coupled with an effective game plan can shrink the "giants" we face down to size.**
    1. Because Christianity is falsifiable, it's also verifiable using facts, evidence, and thoughtful reflection.
    2. The alternate views are burdened by difficulties that can be exposed in a gracious, disarming way by using questions creatively in conversations.
    3. Effectiveness requires that we communicate graciously in a manner that conveys understanding rather than creates conflict.
    4. Even using a gentle but shrewd approach, though, doesn't guarantee results. The outcome is up to the Holy Spirit. We speak, but he does the convincing.

C. **Third, we learned that the key to being an effective ambassador for Christ in a hostile culture is to focus on gardening instead of harvesting.**
    1. Key concept: before there can be any harvest, there always has to be a season of gardening.
    2. Jesus indicated in John 4 that though there was one field and one team, there were two seasons—a gardening season and a harvesting season—and two kinds of workers—gardeners and harvesters.
    3. Gardeners don't try to "close the deal" by force-fitting the gospel into every conversation, but rather seek to "put a stone in someone's shoe." They try to get the other person thinking productively about some compelling aspect of the Christian worldview or some liability in their own view.
    4. Since harvesting is easy when the fruit is ripe, most of our effective effort will be spent in gardening that eventually leads to a fruitful harvest in God's time.
    5. Most Christians are probably gardeners, not harvesters, but they've only been given harvesting tools, so they sit on the bench and out of play.

⟦?⟧ Self-Assessment

Try to answer the following questions without using your notes.

1. What apostle was, surprisingly, frightened into silence, and how was that remedied?

> The apostle was _____, and he was encouraged when Jesus appeared to him and told him not to be _____ but to _____ and not be silent.

2. What was Jesus careful to do before he sent his disciples out on a mission in hostile territory?
    > First, he _____ them, then he _____ them, and then he told them not to be _____.

3. Where is the "street"?
    > The "street" is anywhere you feel _____ or exposed to _____.

4. What do we mean when we say Christianity is falsifiable, and why is that a good thing, not a bad thing?
    > It means that, in principle, Christianity can be shown to be _____ or _____. That's good because it also means that Christianity can be shown to be _____.

5. The *Street Smarts* approach involves using two steps to deal with challenges to your Christian convictions. What are they?
    > First is the _____. You must know the specific _____ of the challenge. Second is the _____. You need to tactfully expose those weaknesses by using specific _____ in a precise manner in conversation.

6. What do we mean when we say the gospel is no longer "simple"?
    > We mean that even though the truth is still the truth, the way people _____ the truth has changed dramatically. The culture has moved on, but our _____ have not.

7. What is a key takeaway from Jesus' parable of the sower in Matthew 13:18–23?
    > When people hear the word that is sown and do not _____ it, the word is quickly snatched away by the devil. When people hear the word and understand it, the word is able to bear _____.

8. What insight is key to having an abundant harvest?
   ▸ Before there can be any _____, there must be a _____ of gardening.

9. What important lesson about evangelism do we learn from Jesus' comments to his disciples in John 4?
   ▸ There is one _____ but two different seasons: a _____ season and a _____ season. There is one _____ but two different types of _____: gardeners and harvesters.

10. What is the specific goal when we garden in individual conversations?
    ▸ Just try to put a _____ in their shoe. Try to give them something to think about instead of trying to _____ the deal by pressing for a decision for Christ.

☑ Self-Assessment with Answers

1. The apostle was **Paul**, and he was encouraged when Jesus appeared to him and told him not to be **afraid** but to **speak** and not be silent.
2. First, he **trained** them, then he **warned** them, and then he told them not to be **afraid**.
3. The "street" is anywhere you feel **vulnerable** or exposed to **danger**.
4. It means that, in principle, Christianity can be shown to be **false** or **disproven**. That's good because it also means that Christianity can be shown to be **true**.
5. First is the **content**. You must know the specific **weaknesses** of the challenge. Second is the **dialogue**. You need to tactfully expose those weaknesses by using specific **questions** in a precise manner in conversation.
6. We mean that even though the truth is still the truth, the way people **hear** the truth has changed dramatically. The culture has moved on, but our **methods** have not.
7. When people hear the word that is sown and do not **understand** it, the word is quickly snatched away by the devil. When people hear the word and understand it, the word is able to bear **fruit**.
8. Before there can be any **harvest**, there must be a **season** of gardening.

9. There is one **field** but two different seasons: a **gardening** season and a **harvesting** season. There is one **team** but two different types of **workers**: gardeners and harvesters.

10. Just try to put a "**stone**" in their shoe. Try to give them something to think about instead of trying to **close** the deal by pressing for a decision for Christ.

Interactive Group Study Questions

1. At the beginning of his time with his disciples, Jesus said, "Follow Me, and I will make you fishers of men." What do you think he meant by this? How do these words encourage you as you work to be a good ambassador for Christ?

2. Discuss the reasons from Matthew 10 why the disciples could trust Jesus when three times he told them not to fear as he sent them out on their first mission trip.

3. No good answer or clever technique will ensure that anyone will turn to Christ. What are some factors that shape a person's beliefs and keep them from genuine conversion?

4. Talk about some of the ways the cultural conversation has changed and become more hostile to Christianity in the past few decades.

5. Discuss the idea of gardening in evangelism. Do you agree with it? Why or why not?

6. How does the one field, two seasons concept (sowing and reaping, gardening and harvesting) and one team with two types of workers concept encourage you as an individual wanting to share the gospel? Do you think you're a gardener or a harvester? Why?

Food for Thought

Bench Time

What happens when a massive number of Christians whom God has gifted as gardeners rather than harvesters are presented with a harvesting model of evangelism that is inconsistent with their spiritual temperament? They sit on the bench, remaining inactive and out of play. When gardeners don't garden for whatever reason, the harvest suffers. Remember the sluggard from Proverbs. He did not plow after autumn, so he reaped nothing when harvesttime came 'round.[6]

Good News, Bad News

The good news should never get the short shrift. Remember, though, that the good news has little weight without the bad news. Most people don't care about insulin, for example, unless they have diabetes.

Often Jesus gave only half his message, letting the bad news—the unbearable burden and impossible obligation of flawless goodness—weigh upon his listeners (see the Sermon on the Mount). Only later, after they were exhausted from shouldering the crushing weight of their own sin, would he say, "Come to Me, all who are weary and heavy-laden, and I will give you rest."[7]

Rest from what? Rest from the burden of the bad news; rest from the hopeless load of striving to be justified by law, a burden Christ was willing and able to lift from their shoulders. That's gospel. Yes, he got to the good news, eventually. But first he gardened.

---

6. Proverbs 20:4.
7. Matthew 11:28.

SESSION 2

QUESTIONS KEEP YOU SAFE

▶ Demonstrating Mastery

Try recalling the answers to the following questions without using your notes. The answers are in the "Self-Assessment with Answers" section of session 1.

1. Where is the "street"?
2. The *Street Smarts* approach involves using two steps to deal with challenges to your Christian convictions. What are they?
3. What is the specific goal when we garden in individual conversations?

I. Review and Looking Ahead

A. In the preceding session, we covered the following:
1. First, we candidly acknowledged that evangelism can be tough in today's culture.
2. Second, we learned that adequate knowledge coupled with an effective game plan can shrink the "giants" we face down to size.
3. Third, we learned that the key to being an effective ambassador for Christ in a hostile culture is to focus on gardening instead of harvesting.

B. **Here is what we'll cover in this session:**
1. First, I'll tell you about the simplest, most effective way to navigate tricky conversations—and it's also the way that will keep you safe in those conversations.
2. Second, I'll sketch out the tactical game plan you'll use to navigate those conversations using questions.
3. Third, I'll talk about four specific ways questions protect you in conversation.
4. Finally, I'll give you a sample dialogue showing exactly how using the tactical questioning approach can make conversations safer for you and more effective with those you engage.

II. Questions Keep You Safe

A. **Having a specific plan is a huge benefit when maneuvering in conversations about Christ.**
1. The key to navigating effectively with others in rough spiritual waters is to use questions.
2. Carefully placed questions are the core of the tactical game plan.

B. **Why questions?**
1. There are many good reasons, but one of the most important ones is this: *questions keep you safe.*
   a. Assertions make you vulnerable. It's easy for someone to simply contradict your assertions or press you to defend your claims.
   b. Questions help you sidestep those liabilities, keeping you out of harm's way yet still allowing you to make progress.
2. When you use questions, you're in the driver's seat of the conversation.
   a. Your questions "steer" the dialogue in the direction you want it to go.
   b. If you're not comfortable with the course your discussion is taking, you can redirect with a question.

Here's where I first got this idea.

C. **Taking a tip from a bumbling detective**
   1. I call this approach "Columbo" after the cagey TV detective who had a clever method of capturing the criminal. Lieutenant Columbo always seemed a bit confused. Yet his polite yet bumbling manner was thoroughly disarming.
   2. Columbo's opening salvo appeared innocuous, but was key to his effectiveness: "Do you mind if I ask you a question?"
      a. The initial query was followed by another, then another, and another. Each answer he received provided another part to the puzzle the lieutenant was piecing together in his mind.
      b. At the end of the episode, Columbo showed his hand and solved the crime.
   3. Asking questions was second nature to Columbo—a habit, he said. Make it your habit, too. Here is the key to Columbo—and the heart of the *Street Smarts* approach: the Christian goes on the initiative in a relaxed, disarming way by using specific questions to move the conversation forward, eventually undermining objections and strengthening the case for Christianity.

Reflect a Moment

Lieutenant Columbo wasn't alone. Jesus used questions constantly, with more than three hundred recorded in the Gospels. Plato's mentor, the ancient philosopher Socrates, regularly questioned his students, probing with what we now call the "Socratic method."

III. Four Ways Questions Increase Your Safety Yet Still Allow You to Make a Difference

A. **First, questions get you going.**
   1. Most people find that starting a spiritual conversation is a little awkward.
      a. Using well-placed questions, though, is a safe way to get off the bench and into conversation.
      b. It helps ease you into the game, so to speak, in a friendly, nonthreatening way.
   2. Sometimes simple questions trigger a longer chat you never intended to have yet bears unexpected spiritual fruit.

B. **An inconvenient conversation I had one morning with a waitress in Seattle is a perfect case in point.**
1. First, you need to know I'm not a morning person.
    a. When I dragged myself into the hotel restaurant that early Sunday morning, I didn't want to talk about anything.
    b. I especially didn't want to talk about God or Jesus or anything spiritual. Too early. The waitress, though, was buoyant and chatty.

"So, what brings you to Seattle this beautiful morning?" she gushed.

"I'm going to preach at a church this morning," I said, thinking that would send her scurrying.

"Oh, that's great!" she said.

Why was that great? I thought. "Are you a Christian?"

"No. I used to be, but now the universe takes care of me."

What could that mean? My inner "Columbo" began to take over. "How can the universe take care of you? Is the universe a person?"

"Oh no," she said confidently.

"Then how can the universe take care of you?"

"Well," she stammered, "uh, I guess I mean that *God* takes care of me. God *is* the universe."

"Is the universe a person?" I had to ask.

"No."

"Then how could God *be* the universe?" I wasn't trying to trap her. I wasn't even trying to witness to her—too early for that. All I was trying to do was make sense of what she was saying.

After more futile attempts by me to get clarity, she finally took my order and drifted off, supremely confident in the soundness of the confusing view of reality that she'd traded Christianity for.

When she dropped my check on the table, though, she paused and said something I did not expect to hear.

"You know, no one has ever asked me questions about my views before," she said, then added, "*and it got me thinking.*"

"Well," I answered with a smile, "if we had more time, I could ask you more questions and you could do more thinking." It was all I had a chance to say.

Fortunately, I had a copy of *The Story of Reality* in my bag.[1] I grabbed it quickly and offered it to her before I left, and she received it with the same energy she had greeted me with earlier.

2. By using simple questions with the waitress, I effortlessly initiated a conversation that God used to put a stone in her shoe *even when I wasn't trying*. Key point: the questions got me going.

> **Ambassador Skills**
>
> There's a reason questions make the initial stages of a conversation much easier. Once you offer a query, it's the other person's turn to respond. All you need to do is listen. It's simple. Once you're rolling, the conversation almost always gets easier as opportunities for more questions present themselves.

C. Second, questions get you valuable "intel."

1. Once on a flight out of LAX, I chatted amiably with a thirtysomething passenger sitting next to me. As I gently drew him out with questions, I learned he was not a Christian, though he used to be.
   a. In fact, he said he used to be a preacher's kid.
   b. What had happened to his preacher dad? "Oh, he's still alive. He's just not a preacher anymore. In fact, he's not a Christian anymore, either."
2. Valuable intel? You bet.
   a. If I'd jumped into the conversation leading with the gospel, I'm sure I would have hit a trip wire.
   b. Questions often reveal obstacles you can carefully maneuver around once you know where they are.
3. Questions can give you the lay of the land so you can avoid the landmines.

---

1. Gregory Koukl, *The Story of Reality* (Grand Rapids: Zondervan, 2017).

D. Third, questions protect you from having to defend your own view.

1. If you're asking questions, you're not making statements.
    a. Since the burden of proof is always on the person making the claim (more on that later), you're in the clear.
    b. If you stick with questions, you have nothing to defend, so you're in a safe place, not vulnerable to counterattack.
2. Holding back a bit before showing your hand is often a smart move.
    a. In some conversations, I wait a long time before jumping in with both feet.
    b. As long as I'm not making my own case, I'm safe. Instead, I ask questions.
        (1) If you're not sure of the best way to maneuver, just ask questions.
        (2) Then listen carefully.
3. Here's my advice.
    a. First, when you're afraid a conversation may get awkward, be patient and listen—a lot.
        (1) Ask lots of clarification questions.
        (2) Wait for the right opportunity before weighing in.
    b. Second, if you see an opening, take whatever God gives you, even if it's less than what you hoped for.
        (1) Don't swing for the fences.
        (2) Just try to make one good point.

> **Ambassador Skills**
>
> Even for those tutored in refuting challenges and objections to Christianity, questions provide a vital element that may be missing for them—a bridge from the content they already know to the interaction they are trying to initiate. It's a shrewd way of spanning that gap and managing conversations.

E. Fourth, questions make exiting easier, so entering is easier, too.

1. Flying home after nearly two weeks of grueling work in Paraguay, I had a midnight layover in São Paulo, Brazil.

  a. I was tired and didn't want to talk. I was also hungry but leery of eating foreign food (I'd recently gotten sick in Uganda).

  b. So I checked the restaurant out with a young American who was speaking fluent Portuguese with the waitress.

2. When I invited him to dine with me, I learned why this young man was fluent in the local language: he was a Mormon missionary.

  a. It was a great opportunity to witness, of course.

  b. To be completely candid, though, I didn't want to endure a night of evangelism with a Mormon at midnight in Brazil after two weeks of talks.

3. Then it dawned on me.

  a. I didn't have to mentally commit myself on the front end to a lengthy bout with a nonbeliever.

  b. If I was willing to simply start with a few questions about this Mormon's own beliefs, I could easily exit the spiritual side of the exchange whenever I ran out of gas.

4. Here is the lesson I learned:

  a. When you know you can always stop the conversation by stopping the questions if things get difficult, you'll be more motivated to start.

  b. Easy out, easy in.

F. **You may be wondering if I make any difference by focusing on questions.**

1. I do. And you will, too.

  a. Questions help you ease into conversations.

  b. They'll give you valuable intel.

  c. They'll help you to sidestep the burden of proof until you're ready to defend your own view.

  d. And they'll make it easy for you to get out when it's time to go.

2. Put simply, questions keep you safe.

Next, I want you to see how questions can form the foundation for an easy-to-use, three-step game plan to get you smoothly and effectively into meaningful spiritual conversations.

IV. The Game Plan

Here's the first step of the game plan:

A. Columbo step one
1. At the beginning of any conversation, focus on one thing and one thing only: *gathering information.* That's all.
    a. Your initial goal is not to answer objections, anticipate challenges, give evidence for Christianity, or even launch into the gospel.
    b. In fact, do not think about anything you might face farther down the road in your chat together. Those concerns will only distract you at this stage. They might even intimidate you into silence.
    c. Instead, all you need to do at first is get the lay of the land. Simply put, you need intel.
        (1) You need a clear picture of exactly what you're up against.
        (2) You need to know the precise complaint, objection, or challenge your friend is offering.
2. Here is a basic model question to help you get going: *What do you mean by that?*
    a. Remember, this is a *model* question.
    b. You might say, for example,
        (1) "I'm a little confused by what you said. What exactly did you mean by that?" or . . .
        (2) "I'm not sure I understand you. Can you clear this up for me?" or . . .
        (3) "Help me out here. What specifically are you getting at?" or . . .
        (4) "Can you give me more detail?" or . . .
        (5) "Are you saying . . . ?" then fill in the blanks.
        (6) Or you can simply say, "Tell me more."
3. Notice that my conversation with the Seattle waitress consisted completely of clarification questions—Columbo #1.
    a. All I was trying to do—somewhat reflexively—was to get clear on her views.
    b. God still was able to use that first, uncomplicated move without my going any further in the game plan than Columbo #1.

4. This initial Columbo question has a number of advantages.
   a. First, when you have some form of this question at the ready, it gives you a simple, safe entry point into what might seem at first to be a daunting encounter.
   b. Second, asking this question immediately tosses the ball back into the other person's court so that he has to take the next step, not you. It gives you a bit of a breather. It buys you some time to sort out your own thoughts.
   c. Third, it clarifies the view for both you *and* your challenger.
      (1) It's important that *you're* completely clear on the other person's view so you don't misrepresent it and take exception to a position the other person doesn't hold.[2]
      (2) It's also important that *they're* clear on their own view—something many critics have not thought carefully about.

Reflect a Moment

One university professor told me that the tactical approach has kept her safe in the hostile environment of the academy while still allowing her to make progress using questions to gently—yet effectively—challenge her colleagues' views.

That's the first step: gather information with some form of the question "What do you mean by that?"

B. **Columbo step two**
   1. The second step of our game plan builds on the information you gathered with the first step.
      a. Once you have a clear picture of *what* a person believes, you'll then want to understand *why* he believes it
      b. You'll want to find out the specific reasons—if he has any—for the view he's advancing.
   2. I call this move reversing the burden of proof.

---

2. Refuting a distortion is not only bad manners; it's bad thinking, an informal fallacy known as a "straw man."

      a. The burden of proof is the responsibility ("burden") someone in the conversation has to give reasons ("proof") for his view.

      b. Here is the basic burden of proof rule: the one who makes the claim bears the burden.

          (1) If a critic says something is so—especially if it's controversial—then it's *his* obligation to give reasons why anyone should take his claim seriously.

          (2) It's not *your* responsibility to refute him—not at first.

3. Here's why this step is so important.

      a. If we allow a challenger to sidestep his responsibility here and instead push the burden back on us ("Prove me wrong") . . .

          (1) We've relieved him of any responsibility to make his case.

          (2) We've given him a free ride.

4. So, here's our rule for Columbo #2: no more free rides.

      a. Every time someone makes a claim—and after you get clear on what he means by his claim (Columbo #1)—ask your second Columbo question, some form of "*How did you come to that conclusion?*"

5. Again, this is a model question. You could also say . . .

      a. "I'm curious, what are your reasons for that?" or . . .

      b. "What gives you confidence your view is actually true?" or . . .

      c. "How exactly does that work?" or . . .

      d. "Why do you think that's the way it happened?"

▶ Reflect a Moment

When you ask your first Columbo questions, you'll frequently get something you did not expect: silence. Dead air. Critics often enter a conversation with their sails filled with bluster, but when asked for even a modest clarification, those sails go slack since they have no idea how to respond. They simply *do not know* what they mean by the issues they raise or the reasons they hold them. They've never thought them through for themselves.

6. Notice that at this stage of the game plan you haven't taken any risk since you haven't advanced your own view.

      a. You've simply used questions to ease into the shallow end of the pool, so to speak.

b. No pressure, no worries. So far, so good.

Step three is more advanced.

C. Columbo step three

1. The final step of the game plan is the main focus of *Street Smarts*, and it's more challenging.
    a. You will not be using questions passively to gather information.
    b. Instead, you'll be using questions actively to convey information of a specific kind.
    c. You'll be using questions to exploit a weakness or a flaw in the other person's view.
2. Which brings us to a speed bump. The final step of the tactical game plan requires three things you may not have:
    a. One, you need to know the weakness or the flaw.
    b. Two, you need insight into what questions to use to expose that liability.
    c. Three, you need a basic blueprint in your mind of the steps you need to take to make your point as the conversation unfolds.
3. This final phase takes you into the deeper end of the pool.
4. No worries. *Street Smarts* will help you with those three steps on a variety of common challenges you'll face as a Christian.

▪ Reflect a Moment

What if you don't see the flaw? Now what? No problem. The first two steps still give opportunity for God to use those simple questions. It happens all the time. If nothing else, you've gotten an education about another's views along with some practice at having a relaxed discussion so that future conversations like this will be easier for you. You can wade into deeper water when you're ready.

D. So, your first task with Columbo #3 is to identify the flaw or weakness in a challenger's point of view.

1. The flaw is the target your questions will be aimed at.

2. Let's say, for example, someone claims there is no God.
    a. I know that a powerful evidence for God's existence is that the universe had a beginning (called the *cosmological argument*).
    b. My plan, then, will be to leverage the scientific evidence for the beginning of the universe to argue that God is the most reasonable cause. That's my target.[3]
3. Once I have my target clearly in view—the specific point I want to make—
    a. I then think about the steps I need to take to get to my conclusion.
    b. I also need to strategize questions I can use to make my point.
4. Here is an example.
    a. Suppose someone says, "Abortion is health care."
    b. Based on that assertion, they begin to make the case for adequate "health care"—abortion—for women, especially those who are poor.
5. I happen to know—and so do you, once you think about it—that killing unborn children has nothing to do with health care.
    a. My target, then, is to show that abortion does not serve anyone's health needs, mother or child.
    b. My questions are going to move the discussion in that direction.
6. For example:

"Abortion shouldn't be illegal. It's health care."
   "Let me ask you a question. What is health care?" [Columbo #1]
"It's care that's provided to make someone healthier, obviously."
   "Good. I agree. But now I have another question. Is pregnancy an illness?"
"Of course not."
   "So, when a woman is pregnant, she's not sick, right?"
"Right."
   "Maybe I'm missing something here, but how can abortion be health care for the mother if the mother is not sick?"
"But pregnancy is a health care concern."

---

3. I realize that precisely *when* the universe began is a matter of debate between Christians, but that discussion is irrelevant to my point here. If the universe *had* a beginning—which is largely established science—then the question of what the adequate *cause* for the universe was is a fair one.

>"I agree, but in the case of abortion, you're not helping a woman have a healthy pregnancy, are you? You're helping her end it, so the woman's health is not an issue, is it? What about the fetus? What does abortion do to the fetus?"
>
>"It kills it. That's the point, isn't it?"
>
>"Right, but then how is abortion health care for the fetus?"

7. Notice what I've done.
    a. I'm aware of a flaw in the claim.
    b. I quickly strategized steps I needed to take to reveal the flaw.
    c. Then I employed a series of questions to expose the flaw.
8. There's something else you may not have noticed, though.
    a. By using questions, I subtly enlisted my challenger as an unwitting partner in helping me unpack the problems with his view.
    b. The dialogue above could easily have been a monologue. When my challenger said, "Abortion is health care," I could have said:

    > Abortion is not health care. Health care helps sick people get better. But pregnancy isn't a sickness, so abortion can't be health care for the mother. Abortion doesn't keep her healthy in pregnancy. It ends her pregnancy by killing the baby, so abortion isn't health care for the baby, either. Therefore, abortion isn't health care.

9. Look what can happen, though, when you use statements rather than questions.

    >"Abortion is not health care. Health care helps sick people get better."
    >
    >*"Not always. Sometimes it keeps them from getting sick."*
    >
    >"But pregnancy isn't a sickness, so abortion can't be health care for the mother."
    >
    >*"Yes, it can be."*
    >
    >"Abortion doesn't keep her healthy in pregnancy."
    >
    >*"It does if she doesn't want to be pregnant."*
    >
    >"It ends her pregnancy by killing the baby, so abortion isn't health care for the baby, either."
    >
    >*"It's not a baby. It's a blob of tissue."*

"Abortion is not health care."

"Yes, it is."

10. See what happened? When you use statements to build your case, your friend can argue with every statement. You get nowhere fast.
11. With the tactical approach, though, using questions instead of assertions . . .
    a. You invite your challenger to provide the same information he might have otherwise disputed.
    b. He then becomes your accomplice by affirming the very points that eventually undermine his view.

> **Ambassador Skills**
>
> Remember, these basic questions will get you started, but you're certainly not limited to them. As you get more effective using the game plan, you'll discover a host of ways to probe effectively with your own questions.

V. What Main Points Did We Cover in This Session?

A. **First, I made the case that the simplest, most effective way to navigate tricky conversations—the way that will also keep you safe—is to use questions.**
   1. Questions protect you from someone simply contradicting your assertions or pressing you to defend your claims.
   2. Questions keep you in the driver's seat of the conversation. Your questions "steer" the interaction in the direction you want it to go. If you're not comfortable with the course the conversation is taking, you can redirect with another question.
   3. Our model—and namesake—for this approach is Lieutenant Columbo. Like Columbo, we're going to adopt the habit of moving forward in conversations by asking questions in a relaxed and disarming way. In our case, our questions will ultimately be designed to—in a legitimate way—either undermine another's contrary point of view or strengthen our case for Christianity.

B. **Second, I shared four specific ways questions help you in conversations.**
   1. One, questions get you going. They provide a safe way to get you off the bench and into a discussion.
   2. Two, questions get you valuable "intel." They reveal the lay of the land so you can avoid emotional landmines.
   3. Three, questions protect you from having to defend your own view. If you're asking questions, you're not making statements, so you shoulder no burden of proof.
   4. Four, with questions it's easier to exit, so it's easier to enter, too. If you know you can stop the conversation by stopping the questions if things get difficult, you'll be more motivated to start. Easy out, easy in.

C. **Next, I sketched out three steps of the tactical game plan to help you navigate conversations using questions.**
   1. First step: gather information using some form of the question "What do you mean by that?"
      a. This question gives you a simple, safe entry point into the conversation.
      b. It tosses the ball back into the other person's court so that he has to make the next move, not you.
      c. It helps clarify the view for both you and your challenger.
   2. Second step: reverse the burden of proof with some form of the question "How did you come to that conclusion?"
      a. Remember, the person who makes the controversial claim has the responsibility to give reasons for his view (the "burden of proof").
      b. You do not have the responsibility to refute him—not at first.
      c. No more free rides
   3. Third step (and the main focus of *Street Smarts*): use questions to expose a weakness or a flaw in the other's view. With this more advanced step . . .
      a. You need to know the weakness or the flaw.
      b. You need insight into what questions to use to expose that liability.
      c. You need a blueprint in your mind of the steps you will take to direct your moves as the conversation unfolds.

D. Finally, I gave you a sample dialogue showing exactly how using the tactical questioning approach can make conversations safer for you and more effective with the other person.

? Self-Assessment

Try to answer the following questions without using your notes.

1. What is the key to navigating effectively with others in rough spiritual waters?
   > The key to navigating effectively with others in rough spiritual waters is to ask_____.

2. Give two reasons why this approach is so effective.
   > One, questions keep you _____.
   > Two, questions keep you in the _____ of the conversation.

3. What do we call this approach based on the name of a famous TV detective?
   > We call this approach the _____ tactic.

4. What two elements of this detective's style make it so effective?
   > He is _____ and _____ because he appears innocuous.

5. In a sentence, what is the key to the Columbo tactic and the heart of the *Street Smarts* approach?
   > The Christian goes on the initiative in a relaxed, disarming way by using specific _____ to eventually _____ objections and strengthen the case for Christianity.

6. List four ways questions increase your safety in conversations yet still allow you to make a difference.
   > First, questions get you _____. Second, questions get you valuable _____. Third, questions protect you from having to _____ your own view. Fourth, questions make _____ easier, so entering is easier, too.

7. What is the first step in the game plan and the model question you'll use?
   > The first step in the game plan is to gather _____. The model question is "What do you _____ by that?"—or some variation.

8. Give three advantages of this first step.
   > One, it provides a simple, safe _____ into the conversation. Two, it tosses the ball in the other person's _____ so that he has to take the next step, not you. Third, it _____ the view for both you and your challenger.

9. What is the second step of the game plan?
   > The second step of the game plan is _____ the _____ of proof.

10. What is the rule that applies to this step?
    > The person who makes the claim bears the burden of _____, that is, providing reasons or _____ that his view is a good one.

11. What happens if you ignore this step?
    > We give the other person a _____ when we don't ask him to defend his view before we try to refute it.

12. What is the model question for Columbo #2?
    > The model question for Columbo #2 is "How did you come to that _____?"—or some variation.

13. What is the third step of the game plan?
    > The third step of the game plan is using questions to _____ a weakness or a _____ in the other person's view.

14. What three things do you need to know to use the third step of Columbo?
    > First, you need to know the _____ or flaw. Second, you need insight into what _____ to use to expose that liability. Third, you need a basic _____ in your mind of the steps you need to take to move forward in the conversation.

☑ Self-Assessment with Answers

1. The key to navigating effectively with others in rough spiritual waters is to ask **questions**.
2. One, questions keep you **safe**. Two, questions keep you in the **driver's seat** of the conversation.
3. We call this approach the **Columbo** tactic.
4. He is **polite** and **disarming** because he appears innocuous.
5. The Christian goes on the initiative in a relaxed, disarming way by using specific **questions** to eventually **undermine** objections and strengthen the case for Christianity.
6. First, questions get you **going**. Second, questions get you valuable "**intel**." Third, questions protect you from having to **defend** your own view. Fourth, questions make **exiting** easier, so entering is easier, too.
7. The first step in the game plan is to gather **information**. The model question is "What do you **mean** by that?"—or some variation.
8. One, it provides a simple, safe **entry point** into the conversation. Two, it tosses the ball in the other person's **court** so that he has to take the next step, not you. Third, it **clarifies** the view for both you and your challenger.
9. The second step of the game plan is **reversing** the **burden** of proof.
10. The person who makes the claim bears the burden of **proof**, that is, providing reasons or **evidence** that his view is a good one.
11. We give the other person a **free ride** when we don't ask him to defend his view before we try to refute it.
12. The model question for Columbo #2 is "How did you come to that **conclusion**?"—or some variation.
13. The third step of the game plan is using questions to **exploit** a weakness or a **flaw** in the other person's view.
14. First, you need to know the **weakness** or flaw. Second, you need insight into what **questions** to use to expose that liability. Third, you need a basic **blueprint** in your mind of the steps you need to take to move forward in the conversation.

📢 Interactive Group Study Questions

1. What is the key to Lieutenant Columbo's detective method (and the heart of the *Street Smarts* approach)? How does following his example benefit Christian ambassadors?
2. Discuss the four ways questions increase your safety yet still allow you to make a difference. Share experiences you've had when using questions helped you.
3. What is the one thing to focus on at the beginning of any conversation? Discuss why it's important to initially keep your focus on this one goal.
4. What is the first Columbo question, and what is its purpose? How can using this question serve you in conversations with nonbelievers? Share examples of times this question has been helpful in your own interactions with others.
5. What is the second Columbo question? Explain how reversing the burden of proof takes the pressure off you in a discussion. Share examples from your life when this step has been helpful.
6. What is the difference between Columbo #1 and #2 and the third step of the game plan? Discuss why this step is more advanced but also more effective.

💡 Going Deeper: Information for Self-Study

1. Think about stepping into the shallow end of the pool using the first two Columbo questions to initiate a few relaxed conversations. Just be a student of the other person's views, not an advocate of your own views. This simple step will help you get into the gardening habit.
2. Be prepared to share your experiences if you are studying with others when you get together next time. Or share one of your experiences with a Christian friend or mentor.

🍎 Food for Thought

Stick with the Plan

My first question (Columbo #1) is designed to give me *valuable information* that sets the stage for what follows. Further inquiries probe the *rationale* for a person's beliefs or objections (Columbo #2). The key to *Street Smarts*, though, is using carefully selected questions to make a point—specifically, to *expose the flaws* in a critic's objections and thus neutralize his challenge (Columbo #3).

During encounters like these, your tactical maneuvers are meant to provide safety for you in conversation while encouraging the objector to think more carefully about his complaints with Christianity or consider problems with his own views he may not have been aware of.

The initial moves are gentle and nonconfrontational, motivated by a genuine curiosity and a desire to understand. They allow you to make tremendous headway in a conversation even when you have zero insight into the challenges you're facing and no skill at verbal maneuvering.

Hold That Thought

Holding back a bit in conversation before showing your hand can rescue you from what might be a premature and awkward conflict of ideas.

For example, in some cases you may not think you have the liberty to express your beliefs as freely as you'd like. Maybe the person you're chatting with is more interested in doing the talking than doing the listening.

No problem. In those situations, here's how to make your job easier. First, ask questions and listen, a lot. Second, after listening, don't swing for the fences. Instead, just try to make one good point stick.

Facing Down the Tough Critic

The toughest critic you will ever face is yourself. Every Christian has doubts at one time or another. That's natural. In *Street Smarts* I want to fortify your confidence that your biblical worldview provides solid answers to your own concerns. I want to give you the assurance you need to have confidence regarding legitimate questions that arise in your own mind. I want to shrink those "giants" down to size for you.

Second, I want to show you how to persuasively put that knowledge into play, leveraging the power of these truths by using specific questions—not statements—to help you navigate shrewdly to gain a substantial tactical advantage in conversations. I want you to be able to give others something concrete and meaningful to think about regarding Jesus and the world he made.

Street Smarts will help you successfully navigate both of these difficulties—your own doubts and also the challenges you'll face from critics.

About Those "Giants"

Just asking questions and listening carefully to the answers will teach you two important lessons. First, non-Christians are not as scary as you thought. They won't loom as large for you once you've talked a bit while showing a genuine interest in their views. Second, challengers are not as smart as you thought, either. The objections—once your critics are pressed to clarify them—are frequently less ominous than you feared.

SESSION 3

INTEL FOR NAVIGATING THE STREET

Demonstrating Mastery

Try recalling the answers to the following questions without using your notes. The answers are in the "Self-Assessment with Answers" section of session 2.

1. What is the key to navigating effectively with others in rough spiritual waters?
2. In a sentence, what is the key to the Columbo tactic and the heart of the *Street Smarts* approach?
3. What are the first, second, and third steps of the game plan?

I. Review and Looking Ahead

A. In the preceding session, we covered the following:
1. First, I made the case that the simplest, most effective way to navigate tricky conversations—the way that will also keep you safe—is to use questions.
2. Second, I shared four specific ways questions help you in conversations.
    a. One, questions get you going. They provide a safe way to get you off the bench and into a discussion.

b. Two, questions get you valuable "intel." They reveal the lay of the land so you can avoid emotional landmines.

   c. Three, questions protect you from having to defend your own view. If you're asking questions, you're not making statements, so you shoulder no burden of proof.

   d. Four, with questions it's easier to exit, so it's easier to enter, too. If you know you can stop the conversation by stopping the questions if things get difficult, you'll be more motivated to start. Easy out, easy in.

3. Next, I sketched out three steps of the tactical game plan to help you navigate conversations using questions.

   a. First step: gather information using some form of the question "What do you mean by that?"

   b. Second step: reverse the burden of proof with some form of the question "How did you come to that conclusion?"

   c. Third step (and the main focus of *Street Smarts*): use questions to expose a weakness or a flaw in the other's view.

4. Finally, I gave you a sample dialogue showing exactly how using the tactical questioning approach can make conversations safer for you and more effective with the other person.

B. Here is what we'll cover in this session:

1. I'll give you specific intel on what you're up against on the street.
2. First, I'll tell you about the nature of the invisible spiritual battle you'll encounter on the street.
3. Second, I'll give you an insight to help you recognize specific spiritual schemes of the devil that are in play in our culture.
4. Third, I'll give you a short tutorial on relativism.

   a. Relativism was the first heresy. It was at the heart of man's rebellion in the garden in the beginning.

   b. Relativism is also the current postmodern heresy. It informs virtually every challenge you'll face on the street today.

II. The Invisible Battlefield

A. **Before we begin dealing with challenges using the third step of our game plan, it's critical that we know exactly what we're facing on the street.**
   1. In military terms this is called *intel*. Good intel gives us the lay of the land before we move forward. To navigate the street effectively, we need to know the spiritual topography of the culture. What exactly are we up against?
   2. I want to give you two important pieces of intel to guide you.
      a. The first will help you understand the chief *spiritual* obstacle you'll encounter on the street.
      b. The second will help you understand the chief *ideological* obstacle you'll face on the street.
   3. The two are connected since the ideological obstacle is a deadly spiritual scheme that originated in the invisible realm.

B. **The unseen realm**
   1. Consider a familiar passage about the spiritual realm that contains an insight you might have missed.

      > Put on the full armor of God, so that you will be able to stand firm against the schemes of the devil. For our struggle is not against flesh and blood, but against the rulers, against the powers, against the world forces of this darkness, against the spiritual forces of wickedness in the heavenly places. (Eph. 6:11–12)

   2. Paul tells us we are in a spiritual battle. You already know this. There is something else, though, you may not have noticed before. Paul also says the devil operates according to specific "schemes"—battle plans, of sorts. I want you to see how that works

C. **Weapon one**
   1. I'd like you to think about four passages in the New Testament that tell us the specific way Satan fights his battles:

> And the great dragon was thrown down, the serpent of old who is called the devil and Satan, *who deceives the whole world.* (Rev. 12:9, emphasis added)

> The god of this world has *blinded the minds of the unbelieving* so that they might not see the light of the gospel of the glory of Christ. (2 Cor. 4:4, emphasis added)

> The Lord's bond-servant must not be quarrelsome, but . . . patient when wronged . . . if perhaps God may grant them repentance leading to the knowledge of the truth, and they may come to their senses and escape from the snare of the devil, *having been held captive by him to do his will.* (2 Tim. 2:24–26, emphasis added)[1]

> *The whole world lies in the power of the evil one.* (1 John 5:19, emphasis added)

🗨 Reflect a Moment

According to the New Testament, the entire world is in the devil's grip. He holds people captive to do his bidding by trickery and deceit. He blinds the minds of those who are perishing. He keeps them from coming to their senses and seeing the truth.

Do not miss this key concept.

2. What is the principal weapon the enemy uses in the spiritual conflict?
    a. It's not power; it's deception. The chief way the devil prevails is by spreading lies.
    b. That means our most potent weapon against him is just the opposite: spreading truth.[2]
        (1) That explains why our first defense against spiritual deception is to gird our loins with *truth* (Eph. 6:14).
        (2) It's why Paul says, "We are destroying *speculations* and every lofty thing raised up against the *knowledge* of God" (2 Cor. 10:5, emphasis added).

---

1. Note, once again, God's vital role in rescuing captive minds and lost souls. You are not left to yourself to unmask the devil's deceptions.
2. This is the reason why defense of truth—apologetics—needs to be a part of any church's spiritual battle strategy.

D. Seeing the Unseen

1. That's the weapon, but what about the schemes? How do we "see" the unseen schemes? Think about this:
   a. People who see will walk around an obvious ditch.
   b. People who are blind will fall right into it since they don't know it's there.
2. The world has been blinded by the devil's lies. That means they're going to fall into spiritual ditches that we can see clearly, but they can't.
3. Here's the "tell," the giveaway:
   a. Look for a big spiritual lie that seems completely obvious to you and other Christians, a massive ditch that can't be missed.
   b. Yet those in the world can't see it. Because they are spiritually blind, they fall right in.

Reflect a Moment

If you wonder why anyone would buy into an obvious spiritual error, if you catch yourself saying, "This makes no sense," then you've probably stumbled onto a demonic scheme. The only explanation for such lack of spiritual perception is spiritual blindness—and we now know who is responsible for that.

Here are some examples:

E. Two schemes

1. Scheme #1
   a. What is the only religion in our culture that has the suffix "phobia" attached to it to protect it from criticism?
      (1) Buddha-phobia? Hindu-phobia? Jew-phobia? Christian-phobia? Hardly.
      (2) Only Islam—Islamophobia
   b. Why is this significant? Because Islam is currently the most dangerous religion in the world, yet lots of people believe Islam is a religion of peace.
      (1) Of course, there are multitudes of kind, generous, peaceful Muslims—especially those you'll likely meet in your community.
      (2) Nevertheless, hardly a week passes when there's not an act of Islamic violence somewhere in the world. Yet any public criticism of Islam is labeled bigotry.

(3) Keep in mind that much of the Islamic world is fiercely opposed to Judaism and Christianity.

2. Scheme #2

   a. The second scheme—one I will cover in depth in the second half of this session—has been around for a long time. It's the claim that there is no truth.

   b. The flaw is so obvious and looms so large that, ironically, many miss it.

      (1) When people say there is no truth, I ask, "Is that true?" See the problem?

      (2) You can also see how the idea that there is no truth cuts the legs out from under Christianity.

3. Notice the pattern in both schemes.

   a. Something of spiritual significance is going on in the visible realm that is obviously false, yet the rank and file cannot see it.

   b. Each is a scheme to blind and deceive regarding something spiritually significant.

F. **If you want to see the unseen . . .**

   1. Look for something spiritually important going on in the visible realm that is so obvious that everyone else should see it, but they don't.

   2. That's the tip-off that you're dealing with something the enemy has doubled down on.

Reflect a Moment

We are in a spiritual battle. The devil holds the whole world in his power. He blinds people from the truth using deception and lies. Spiritual warfare, then, is not principally a power encounter against the forces of darkness, but rather a truth encounter against their lies. Our chief weapon in this battle against lies is truth.

One lie is at the center of Satan's schemes, informing virtually everything you'll face on the street. It's not a new deception, though. It was the very first lie.

III. Relativism, the Primal Heresy

A. **At the beginning . . .**

   1. In the beginning, humans knew no lies, of course.

a. Their realm was ruled by goodness and truth—God's truth.
   b. Then a deceiver intruded. When God's truth was challenged, a counterfeit truth took the stage.
 2. "Has God said?" was the devil's challenge (Gen. 3:1).

   > He's lying. He's holding out on you. He's not good. What do *you* want? What does *your* heart tell you? Truth is not out there. Truth is within. Make your own rules. Follow your own heart. Be true to your own self. Be like God.[3]

 3. At the fall, an alternative "truth" prevailed: the truth within, "my truth."
   a. Note that the revolt in the garden was a rejection of the *external* source of truth—God's truth—in exchange for an *internal* authority—man's truth. God's rule was replaced by self-rule.
   b. This outside/inside distinction—God's truth of the "outside" world versus individual truth on the "inside"—is the root of relativism. I call it the primal heresy because it was at the heart of the first sin.
 4. Relativism is the heartbeat of our age, the pulse of the street.
   a. Every generation has fallen prey to it in one form or another.
   b. This generation, though, celebrates it and idolizes it.

▩ Reflect a Moment

The promise of self-rule is an empty one, of course. The self can only rule when the powers that be allow it to rule. More capable "self-rulers" always enslave the weaker ones, sooner or later. Eventually, relativists become victims of their own devices, just like in the garden.

Here is a brief tutorial to help you understand relativism.

B. Inside or outside?
 1. The word *relativism* refers to a particular understanding of what it means when we say that a belief, a statement, or a point of view is *true*.
 2. When I tutor students on the meaning of truth, I make a dramatic display of placing a pen on the podium. Then I make a statement and ask two questions.

---
3. This, of course, is an interpretative paraphrase of Genesis 3:1–5.

a. Statement: "The pen is on the podium."
   b. First question: "Is the statement true?" The students nod.
   c. Second question (the critical one): "What *makes* the statement true?"
3. Hands shoot up.
   a. "Because I see it there."
      (1) "But if you didn't see it, wouldn't it still be true that the pen is on the podium?"
      (2) "Seeing might help you *know* the statement is true, but it isn't what *makes* it true."
   b. "Because I believe it."
      (1) "But if you stopped believing it, would the pen disappear? I doubt it."
      (2) "Would believing really hard make a pen materialize on top of an empty podium? Probably not."
4. "The thing that makes the statement 'The pen is on the podium' a true statement is a pen and a podium, and the former resting on the latter."
   a. "It doesn't matter if anyone *sees* it."
   b. "It doesn't matter if anyone *believes* it."
   c. "It doesn't matter what anyone thinks at all."
5. The truth of the statement "The pen is on the podium" is completely independent of any person's thoughts. It is, in other words, mind independent.
6. Notice something important: the students' first two responses tie the notion of truth to what is happening on the *inside* of them—their personal belief or individual sensation of seeing—and not on anything that's happening *outside* of them.
   a. This inside/outside distinction is the key to understanding any form of relativism.
   b. It's the difference between subjective truth (truth based on what's on the inside) and objective truth (truth based on what's on the outside).

▶ Reflect a Moment

In the real world, simply believing something cannot make it true. Mere belief cannot change a single thing about the way the world is. If you don't believe in gravity, for example, you will not float away. That is the folly of letting beliefs on the inside define truth.

7. Here is another way of thinking about it:
   a. If the truth you have in mind can change simply by changing your mind, then the basis for that "truth" is only in your mind. It's not in the world.[4]
      (1) The truth is based on something in you as a subject—something on the inside, not on something on the outside.
      (2) That's relativism.
   b. If the truth you have in mind cannot change simply by changing your mind, then the basis for that "truth" is not in your mind.
      (1) The truth is based on something in the world as an object—something on the outside, not something on the inside.
      (2) That's objectivism.

▶ Reflect a Moment

Objectivism is the commonsense, garden-variety understanding of the meaning of the word *truth*. When my philosopher friend Frank Beckwith was asked for the definition of truth, he said, "Do you want the true definition or the false one?" You get the point.

C. Real bad or feel bad?

This inside/outside distinction applies in the same way to morality.

1. With *objective* morality, moral claims are like the statement "The pen is on the podium." They are true based on something outside the person—specific actions or behaviors that are either moral or immoral.
   a. Objective moral truth, like all genuine truth, is always mind independent.
   b. When an objectivist says, "Abortion is wrong," he's talking about abortion itself, the action or conduct in the external world. He's not talking about his internal feelings or preferences about abortion.[5]
2. With *relativistic* morality, moral truth is not dependent on something outside a person. Rather, what's inside them—their personal beliefs, tastes, or preferences—determines if an act is right or wrong.

---

4. I owe this insight to my dear friend J. Warner Wallace.
5. He may have beliefs, feelings, and the like about abortion, of course, but that's not what he's describing.

a. In relativism, no behavior is right or wrong in itself. It's right or wrong only if someone believes it's right or wrong.
   b. That's why people say, "Abortion may be wrong for you, but it's not wrong for me."
3. In relativism, things like abortion, premarital sex, and homosexuality are wrong only if a person thinks it's wrong *for them*.
   a. Morality is up to the individual.
   b. Right and wrong are determined by what's on the inside, not by what's on the outside.

Reflect a Moment

Simply put, a truth is a fact. When we say something is true, generally we mean that our statement matches what is real in the world. The opposite of truth is falsehood. Any claim about the world—even a religious or moral claim—is either true or false. There is no middle ground.

D. **The triumph of the self**
   1. This cultural swing toward self—the "primal heresy," just like back in the garden—began over a century ago but shifted into high gear in the 1960s. Now it has taken over everything.
   2. Today a single slogan sums up the ruling dogma: "You do you."
      a. Two personal pronouns and a verb. Nothing else. The mantra is completely self-reflexive: me about me.
      b. Some have called it "expressive individualism."[6]
   3. On the street, meaning, purpose, and identity are all determined by what's on the inside—what an individual feels, wants, or believes about himself.
   4. Consider, for example, how gender is now viewed.
      a. "Gender" no longer refers to anything about our bodies on the outside.
      b. Rather, gender is completely a matter of preference and personal self-determination on the inside. Living what you believe about yourself is now called "being authentic."

---

6. Carl Trueman, *The Rise and Triumph of the Modern Self* (Wheaton, IL: Crossway, 2020), 46.

5. The slogan on a Ninja Warrior T-shirt reads, "Be your own hero." Think about that.
   a. Heroes are ones we look up to because of some superior virtue.
      (1) Being your own hero means the self is the high-water mark.
      (2) Thus, hero worship is reduced to self-worship.
   b. That is what you're up against on the street.
6. Here's why this insight matters.
   a. If you don't understand how thoroughly the primal heresy permeates the current culture, you will not understand the hostility this generation has toward Christianity.
   b. To them, the objective-truth-that-applies-to-everyone Christianity is postmodern heresy.

Reflect a Moment

A pandemic of narcissism besieges us and is championed as central to individual meaning and personal identity. Self-love and unrestrained pursuit of self-interest are no longer vices; they are virtues. Indeed, they are now considered inviolable human rights.

E. Mordor in our midst
   1. When our first parents exchanged the external rule of God and the objective truth of his world "out there" for the internal rule of their own desires "in here"—the outside/inside exchange at the heart of all forms of relativism—they plunged humanity into darkness.
   2. That first lie informs and influences virtually everything you will face on the street . . .
      a. From views on religion and the existence of God to ideas about sex, marriage, and gender; to views on abortion, Scripture, and God's authority over our lives, etc.
      b. Be prepared. Gird your loins with truth. That is the first step in the battle for human souls.
      c. This task—knowing the truth and defending it—is what the remaining sessions of *Street Smarts* will be devoted to.

IV. What Main Points Did We Cover in This Session?

A. First, I talked about the nature of the invisible spiritual battle you'll encounter on the street.
   1. The devil holds the world in his power.
   2. He does this by blinding the minds of unbelievers with lies.
   3. Our first line of defense against the devil's schemes is to counter his lies with the truth.

B. Second, I gave you some insight on how to recognize the devil's schemes in play in our culture.
   1. Look for a big spiritual lie that seems completely upside down to us, for example, "Islam is a religion of peace" or "There is no truth."
   2. Yet the world is blind and can't see it, so non-Christians fall right into the ditch and buy the lie.

C. Third, we had a short tutorial on relativism.
   1. I call it the "primal heresy" because it was the first sin that broke the world.
   2. In the garden, man traded God's truth for his own individual truth.
   3. This is the difference between objectivism and relativism (aka subjectivism).
      a. When truth is defined by something in the external, mind-independent world God made, that's called *objectivism*.
      b. When truth is defined by something in a person's own mind, that's called *relativism*.
   4. The same outside/inside principle applies to moral truth.
      a. Moral objectivism is the view that actions are right or wrong in themselves regardless of anyone's opinion to the contrary. They are mind independent.
      b. Moral relativism is the view that actions are right or wrong based entirely on what individuals believe about the actions *for them*. They are mind dependent.
      c. This is why the same action could be wrong for some people but right for others, even though their objective circumstances are exactly the same.
   5. Relativism—what some have called "expressive individualism" and manifests itself in slogans like "You do you" and "Be your own hero"—is the mentality that now rules the street.

[?] Self-Assessment

Try to answer the following questions without using your notes.

1. What important detail about spiritual warfare do we discover in Ephesians 6:12?
    - Ephesians 6:12 teaches that Satan wages warfare according to specific _____ or battle plans.

2. What do we learn from four New Testament passages that tell us about Satan's hold on unbelievers?
    - The devil _____ the whole world (Rev. 12:9). He has _____ the _____ of unbelievers (2 Cor. 4:4). He holds them _____ to do his will (2 Tim. 2:26). Consequently, the whole world lies in the power of the evil one (1 John 5:19).

3. What is the number one weapon the devil uses to wage spiritual battle?
    - The principal weapon in the devil's arsenal is not _____, but _____.

4. What kind of encounter, then, is the chief element in spiritual warfare?
    - Spiritual warfare is not so much a _____ encounter against the forces of darkness as it is a _____ encounter against their lies.

5. Considering the profound spiritual blindness of unbelievers, what is one way to recognize a scheme of the devil?
    - Look for something spiritually significant going on in the _____ realm that is so obvious that everyone else should _____ it, but they don't.

6. What was the "primal heresy," the first sin in the garden?
    - The first sin in the garden was a rejection of the ____ source of truth, God's truth, in exchange for an ____ authority, man's truth. God's rule was replaced by ____-rule.

7. What does the word *relativism* refer to?
    - The word *relativism* refers to a particular understanding of what it means when we say that a belief, a statement, or a point of view is _____.

8. What is the basic distinction between objectivism and relativism? Identify it, then describe it as best you can.
   ▸ The basic distinction between objectivism and relativism is called the _____/_____ distinction. Truth based on what's on the _____ is called _____ (relativistic) truth. Truth based on what's on the _____ is called _____ truth. Subjective truth is mind _____. Objective truth is mind _____.

9. Describe moral relativism.
   ▸ In moral relativism, an act is only wrong if the individual _____ it's wrong for him. Right and wrong are determined by beliefs on the _____, not by facts on the _____.

10. Describe the main relativistic slogan guiding culture today.
    ▸ The main relativistic slogan guiding culture today is "_____ do _____."

☑ Self-Assessment with Answers

1. Ephesians 6:12 teaches that Satan wages warfare according to specific **schemes** or battle plans.
2. The devil **deceives** the whole world (Rev. 12:9). He has **blinded** the **minds** of unbelievers (2 Cor. 4:4). He holds them **captive** to do his will (2 Tim. 2:26). Consequently, the whole world lies in the power of the evil one (1 John 5:19).
3. The principal weapon in the devil's arsenal is not **power**, but **deception**.
4. Spiritual warfare is not so much a **power** encounter against the forces of darkness as it is a **truth** encounter against their lies.
5. Look for something spiritually significant going on in the **visible** realm that is so obvious that everyone else should **see** it, but they don't.
6. The first sin in the garden was a rejection of the **external** source of truth, God's truth, in exchange for an **internal** authority, man's truth. God's rule was replaced by **self**-rule.
7. The word *relativism* refers to a particular understanding of what it means when we say that a belief, a statement, or a point of view is **true**.

8. The basic distinction between objectivism and relativism is called the **inside/outside** distinction. Truth based on what's on the **inside** is called **subjective** (relativistic) truth. Truth based on what's on the **outside** is called **objective** truth. Subjective truth is mind **dependent**. Objective truth is mind **independent**.
9. In moral relativism, an act is only wrong if the individual **believes** it's wrong for him. Right and wrong are determined by beliefs on the **inside**, not by facts on the **outside**.
10. The main relativistic slogan guiding culture today is "**You** do **you**."

Interactive Group Study Questions

1. What is the principal weapon Satan uses in the spiritual conflict? Discuss some ways you can see this pattern in play in our culture.
2. Given that Satan uses deception and lies to advance his schemes, what is the Christian's most potent weapon? How does this change your view of spiritual warfare?
3. What are indications that help us to "see" Satan's unseen schemes? Discuss some examples of big spiritual lies you have encountered in society today that seem to follow the "schemes" pattern.
4. How does relativism differ from objectivism? What are the chief characteristics of each? Discuss why Greg calls it the "primal heresy."
5. How does understanding the "inside/outside" distinction help us distinguish between objective truths and subjective truths?

Going Deeper: Information for Self-Study

1. Pay attention to the messages you hear on the street—in advertisements, song lyrics, movie themes, and so on—and see if you can find examples of issues with spiritual or moral significance where people's beliefs are simply upside down but they don't see it. When you find it, take note: it's likely a result of a deceitful scheme of spiritual forces of darkness in heavenly places.
2. Pay attention for the subtle ways that individual feelings and "living your truth"—the primal heresy—are championed as the guide to authenticity, happiness, and self-fulfillment.

3. Be prepared to share what you discovered with those in your group or a trusted Christian friend or mentor when you get together next time.

 Food for Thought

Truth or Power?

History is testimony to a basic fact. Human lives will be ruled by one of two fundamental forces: either truth or power. Humanity will be governed either by the physical facts of God's world and the moral facts of his character or by the forces that oppose those moral and physical facts.

I learned this painful lesson firsthand in my own travels in 1976 behind what was then called the "Iron Curtain." I was encouraging Christians in five communist countries who were being crushed under the hammer of Soviet-style Marxism.[7] The official newspaper of the Communist Party in the Soviet Union at that time was called *Pravda*. The word means "truth." Truth, though, was not a valued commodity under Soviet totalitarianism. Truth was just a wax-nosed propaganda tool used to serve a different end. Power, not truth, was the ultimate instrument of Soviet influence.

Without truth, brute force will always be the master, and freedom to choose to live by truth will be the casualty. Humans will then be compelled to live by lies, and today lies abound.

Despots at the Gates

Aristotle said that all law rests on the necessary foundation of morality. When moral truth is relative, the foundation is gone, and nothing remains but brute force. When truth ceases to provide a protective rampart, totalitarianism is not far behind. Lies, of course, are subversions of truth, and when we live by them, liberty is soon lost.

Don't Believe Them

When people say there is no truth, I often wonder how they want me to respond to their statement. I think they want me to believe them, but the minute I consider the possibility that they might be onto something—the minute I start agreeing with them,

---

7. My experiences in the Soviet bloc were the subject of the article "Iron Curtain Diary," *Stand to Reason*, January 1, 2021, www.str.org/w/iron-curtain-diary.

in other words—I run into a problem. I cannot give the nod to their assertion, since that would be the same thing as saying their view is true, which is the one thing they will not allow me to say.

You see the problem. You can also see how the idea that there is no truth cuts the legs right out from under the Great Commission.

SESSION 4

ATHEISM: THE BEST EXPLANATION FOR THE WAY THINGS ARE?

Demonstrating Mastery

Try recalling the answers to the following questions without using your notes. The answers are in the "Self-Assessment with Answers" section of session 3.

1. What is the number one weapon the devil uses to wage spiritual battle?
2. What was the "primal heresy," the first sin in the garden?
3. What is the basic distinction between objectivism and relativism? Identify it, then describe it as best you can.
4. Describe the main relativistic slogan guiding culture today.

I. Review and Looking Ahead

A. In the preceding session, we covered the following:
1. First, I talked about the nature of the invisible spiritual battle you'll encounter on the street. The devil holds the world in his power, and he does this by blinding the minds of unbelievers with lies. So our first line of defense against the devil's schemes is to counter his lies with the truth.

2. Second, I gave you some insight on how to recognize the devil's schemes in play in our culture. Look for a big spiritual lie that seems completely upside down to us, for example, "Islam is a religion of peace" or "There is no truth." Yet the world is blind and can't see it, so the non-Christians fall right into the ditch and buy the lie.
3. Third, we had a short tutorial on relativism.
    a. I call it the "primal heresy" because it was the first sin that broke the world. In the garden, man traded God's truth for his own individual truth.
    b. This is the difference between objectivism and relativism (aka subjectivism)
        (1) When truth is defined by something in the external, mind-independent world God made, that's called *objectivism*.
        (2) When truth is defined by something in a person's own mind, that's called *relativism*.
    c. The same outside/inside principle applies to moral truth.
        (1) Moral objectivism is the view that actions are right or wrong in themselves regardless of anyone's opinion to the contrary. They are mind independent.
        (2) Moral relativism is the view that actions are right or wrong based entirely on what individuals believe about the actions *for them*. They are mind dependent.
        (3) This is why the same action could be wrong for some people but right for others, even though their objective circumstances are exactly the same.
    d. Relativism—what some have called "expressive individualism" and manifests itself in slogans like "You do you" and "Be your own hero"—is the mentality that now rules the street.

B. Here is what we'll cover in this session:
1. First, I'll explain why the God question is the most important question anyone can answer.
2. Second, I'll address four distractions atheists offer that will throw you off track if you're not careful.
    a. They redefine atheism to avoid having to give evidence for their view.
    b. They redefine faith to keep you from giving evidence for theism.

c. They claim there is no evidence for God, so belief in him is irrational.

d. They challenge you with the "one less God" maneuver.

3. Third, I'll show why God is "the best explanation for the way things are" by offering two of the most powerful reasons the smart money is on theism, not atheism.

a. The cosmological argument based on the existence of the universe

b. The teleological argument based on the dazzling design and order in the universe

II. Atheism: Distractions

A. The existence of God is the most decisive issue in life because the answer to that question sets the course for everything that follows.

1. Dealing with the God question is a kind of structural starting point for everything else.

a. On a materialistic, atheistic view of the universe, things just *are*. Nothing more.

b. No explanation for anything important. No purpose for anything significant.[1]

2. All the big questions, then—issues of origin, meaning, morality, and destiny—and all the secondary concerns, too—for example, questions about sex, gender, liberty, equality, and bodily rights—eventually come down to one question:

a. Are we our own, or do we belong to Someone else?

(1) Either the creature is in charge or the Creator is. Either the Potter calls the shots or the clay does.

(2) If there is no God, then all is clay and nothing but clay.

3. Thus, the God question is the first one to answer since it's the foundation for the answers to all the other questions.

▰ Reflect a Moment

Atheism explains nothing. It is the ultimate non-explanation, "explaining" by denying that explanations exist. "Why is there something rather than nothing?" No reason. "What

---

1. Individual atheists may push back on this characterization ("That's not what *I* believe"), but often that's because they have not carefully considered the ramifications of their view that God does not exist.

caused everything?" Nothing. "What accounts for Morality?" There is no Morality to account for. "Why is there Evil in the world?"[2] There is no real Evil in the world since there is no real morality. "What is wrong with the world?" Nothing. It just is. "How do we fix the world?" We can't fix what's not broken. We can only make the world more consistent with our personal preferences.

III. Four Moves

A. I want to start by giving you insight into four distractions you're likely to face with your atheist friends.
   1. In each case, I'll give you tactical questions—embedded in sample dialogues—to help you move forward yet with minimal risk.
   2. Keep in mind that the goal here is not to close the deal. We're not in harvest mode. We're gardening, using a few simple questions to get you going and to get your friend thinking.

> **Ambassador Skills**
>
> Before I go farther, here's a general maneuver. My first response when somebody tells me he's an atheist is, "That's interesting. What kind of atheist are you?" (Columbo #1). Atheists do not agree on everything. Most are materialists—convinced that nothing exists except physical things governed by natural law[3]—but not all are. Some believe in objective morality; some do not. Some flutter back and forth between atheism and agnosticism, depending on the definitions.

---

2. I capitalize "Morality" here because I mean *deep* morality—*objective* morality as opposed to some individual or cultural make-me-up that satisfies self-interest for the moment. By "Evil" I mean a true violation of Morality, what people have always meant when they raise the problem of evil against God.

3. This view is also called *physicalism* or *naturalism*.

B. First distraction: redefining atheism
1. Oddly, many atheists apparently no longer believe there is no God. Instead, they say they merely lack belief in God.
   a. You might call this "atheism lite."
      (1) They don't claim God *doesn't* exist.
      (2) Rather, they simply have no belief that he does exist.
   b. These atheists are not unbelievers, then. They are simply nonbelievers.
      (1) Since a nonbelief is not a claim, atheists don't have to defend it.
      (2) Therefore, atheism is the default view of reasonable people. That's the rhetorical strategy in play here.
2. Here's the flaw:
   a. Atheists may lack a belief *in* God, but they do not lack a belief *about* God.
      (1) They are believers of a certain kind.
      (2) They believe there is no God. That's why they're called atheists.
   b. The root word *theism* means the existence of God, and the prefix *a* is a negation. An atheist, then, is one who holds "not God," or "God is not."
3. Yes, there's a difference between nonbelief and unbelief, but that's no refuge for the atheist. Here's why:
   a. If you asked me which rugby team was the best one in England, I wouldn't know where to start. I have no information, so I have no opinion. I'm truly a nonbeliever on that question. I'm neutral.
   b. Atheists are not neutral on God, though.
      (1) If they were, they wouldn't be writing books, doing debates, or arguing with Christians.
      (2) No one debates about their nonbeliefs. There'd be nothing to talk about. Atheists argue there is no God. That's hardly a nonbelief.

▶ Reflect a Moment

Richard Dawkins is currently the world's most famous atheist. He makes his case in his bestselling book *The God Delusion*. If God is really a delusion, then he does not exist. Simple. Theists say there is a God, and atheists like Dawkins contend they're wrong—even delusional. Thus, atheists argue that *there is no God*—hardly a nonbelief.

4. Here's the simple solution to this challenge. There are only three possible responses to the claim that God exists.[4]
   a. You can affirm it ("God *does* exist").
   b. You can deny it ("God does *not* exist").
   c. Or you could withhold judgment ("I'm neutral"), either for lack of information or lack of interest.
5. With that insight in place, here's how I'd engage an atheist who makes this move:

> "The way you describe your atheism confuses me a bit. Would you mind if I ask you a few questions?"

"No. Go ahead."

> "I'm going to make a statement, and I'd like to hear your response to it. Okay?"

"Sure."

> "Here it is: God exists. What do you personally believe about that statement?"

"I'm agnostic. I lack a belief in God."

> "Well, agnostics have no opinion one way or the other. From what you've said so far, though, it doesn't sound like you're neutral on God. Maybe I can put the question another way."

"Okay."

> "Given the statement 'God exists,' you have three choices. You could affirm the statement (that would be my view, theism), you could deny the statement (that would be atheism), or you could completely withhold judgment since you have no opinion one way or another (that would be agnosticism). So, do you affirm the statement 'God exists,' do you deny that God exists, or do you have no opinion one way or another?"

"Like I said, I lack a belief in God."

> "I get that. But just to be clear, that wasn't one of the options. Are you saying you have no opinion one way or another? Are you sitting on the fence on the God issue?"

---

4. I owe this insight to my philosopher friend Doug Geivett.

"I have no belief in God."

"Okay, let me put it this way. I believe in God, but you've been pushing back on that. You think I'm mistaken, right?"

"Right."

"So, if you think I'm wrong about God existing, then you must believe he doesn't exist, which is why you have no belief in God. Does that make sense?"

6. The purpose here is to even the playing field a bit. Both Christians and atheists have beliefs—and those beliefs are at odds. That means each has a view to defend.

7. Don't give the atheist a free ride here by letting him get away with the "I simply lack belief in God" move.
   a. He *does* have a belief *about* God.
   b. His belief *about* God is that God does not exist.

C. Second distraction: redefining "faith"

1. The atheist's first maneuver keeps him from having to defend his *own* view. His second move is an attempt to keep you from defending *your* view.
   a. Atheist Peter Boghossian's approach is typical:

   > If one had sufficient evidence to warrant belief in a particular claim, then one wouldn't believe the claim on the basis of faith. "Faith" is the word one uses when one does not have enough evidence to justify holding a belief.[5]

   b. Boghossian then redefines faith as "pretending" (his word).[6]
2. On this view, faith and evidence are at opposite ends of the spectrum.
   a. If you have one, you can't have the other.
   b. That's the way atheists almost universally characterize faith these days.

---

5. Peter Boghossian, *A Manual for Creating Atheists* (Durham, NC: Pitchstone, 2013), 23.
6. Boghossian, 24. Find my full response to Boghossian's project in "Tactics for Atheists," Stand to Reason, May 1, 2019, www.str.org/w/tactics-for-atheists.

3. But this simply is not the Christian view. It's a straw man.[7] Let me say, respectfully, that . . .
   a. It does not matter how atheists like Boghossian define faith.
   b. It does not matter how some misinformed *Christians* define faith, either (many make this same mistake).
   c. It only matters how *Christianity* defines faith.
4. The biblical accounts are replete with appeals to evidence to justify Christianity's claims.[8] Listen to this summary the apostle John gives at the end of his gospel (John 20:30–31):

   > Therefore many other signs [miracles] Jesus also performed in the presence of the disciples, which are not written in this book; but these have been written so that you may believe that Jesus is the Christ, the Son of God; and that believing you may have life in His name.

   a. John says that the entire purpose of his gospel is to give evidence for faith in Christ.
   b. John makes no appeal to blind faith here.
5. Biblical faith means active trust, and in Scripture this trust is based on reasons and evidence, not blind leaps. Note these passages:
   a. Acts 2:22 (emphasis added): "Jesus the Nazarene, a man *attested to you* by God with *miracles and wonders and signs* . . ."
   b. Acts 1:3 (emphasis added): "To these [apostles] He also presented Himself alive after His suffering, by *many convincing proofs* . . ."
   c. John 10:38 (emphasis added): "Though you do not believe Me, *believe the works* [that is, miracles], *so that you may know* and understand that the Father is in Me."

---

7. A "straw man" is an informal fallacy in which someone mischaracterizes a view and then easily defeats the misrepresentation.

8. Whether a critic believes the accounts or not isn't relevant to my point: since the Bible offers reasons for faith, biblical faith is not blind. A skeptic may not find those reasons persuasive, but that's a different matter.

d. Acts 17:2–3 (emphasis added): "And according to Paul's custom, he . . . *reasoned* with them from the Scriptures, explaining and *giving evidence* that the Christ had to suffer and rise again from the dead."

6. Put simply, *according to Scripture*, biblical faith is not a blind leap, but a step of trust based on good reasons.

7. Here's a sample dialogue:

> "It's obvious we have different definitions of faith here. That's okay, but since we're talking about my view right now, maybe we can use my definition."
>
> "What's that?"
>
> "Biblical faith is trust based on reasons and evidence. It's not a leap."
>
> "Well, I still think faith is blind."
>
> "What if I gave you evidence for my beliefs. What then?"
>
> "Then it's not faith."
>
> "What would you call it?"
>
> "I don't know. I just know it's not faith if you have reasons."
>
> "Okay, since I'm glad to offer reasons for my views, what word would you like me to use instead?"
>
> "Uh . . . *convictions*?"
>
> "That works for me. So how about I talk about my convictions and the reasons I have for them, then you can respond?"

8. Notice, I'm not going to fuss too much about this definition. I'd rather spend my time giving evidence. He can call that whatever he wants.

D. Third distraction: claiming that belief in God is irrational because there is no evidence.

1. One reason atheists insist that Christian faith is blind is that they're convinced there is no evidence for God, so belief in him must be an irrational leap.

2. The easiest way to get clarity on the "irrational" and "no evidence" charges is to ask some questions.

a. Here's my first one: "Precisely what is irrational about belief in God?" (Columbo #1).

(1) Here, I'm looking for specifics.

(2) It's not enough for an atheist to say, "It's just dumb."

(3) I want him to tell me exactly what's "dumb" about it.

b. Here are a few more questions—in dialogue form—for the atheist.

"What specific arguments for God have you thought about?"

"I haven't seen any."[9]

"Well, if you haven't interacted with the arguments for God, how do you know there's no evidence?"

"Well, I have considered some of them."

"Good. Which ones have you thought about, and what, in your opinion, is wrong with them? How, specifically, have they failed?"

3. You might even ask, "What would count as legitimate evidence for God, in your mind?" This question helps you know if your friend is even open to hearing reasons.

4. The key here is not to settle for vague generalities.

a. Ask your atheist friend to spell out the specific problems he sees with belief in God.

b. You want him to be clear and precise on the exact reasons he believes belief in God is unreasonable.

🔖 Reflect a Moment

If an atheist is convinced there is no evidence for theism, then he thinks his view wins by default since it's the only alternative to atheism—in rational terms, either A or non-A, either God or not God. The approach is appealing to the atheist since, as with the redefinition of the word *faith*, it makes his job easier by allowing him to avoid having to give independent evidence for his view.[10]

---

9. Arguments for God abound, and tomes have been written detailing them, including rationales based on the origin of the universe, design of all sorts, objective morality, well-documented miracles, and Jesus' resurrection—to name just a few.

10. In my estimation, there simply are no good arguments for atheism, thus the distractions: pushing the burden of proof onto the theist by redefining atheism as lack of belief, and charging that theism is irrational or without evidence.

Atheism: The Best Explanation for the Way Things Are? ■ 71

E. Here's one final distraction. I call it the "one less God" maneuver.
  1. With this move, the atheist makes an observation.
     a. He points out that Christians don't believe in other gods like Zeus, Apollo, Amon Ra, Baal, Thor, or the like.
     b. Then he says that he just believes in *one less god* than we do. So Christians are basically atheists, too.
  2. Frankly, I think this is a silly maneuver, but it has stumped a lot of Christians.
     a. To show you how pointless this attempt is, think of these claims:
        (1) All married men are basically bachelors since they're not married to every other woman on the planet.
        (2) People with jobs are basically unemployed since there are gazillions of other companies they don't work for.
        (3) Murderers are basically peaceful folk, considering all the people they haven't killed.
     b. Like I said, silly. That atheists believe in one less god than we do is the difference between an atheist and a theist. That difference makes all the difference. Nothing tricky here.
  3. Here's how I'd address this move in a conversation:

"You're basically an atheist like me."

"What do you mean?" [Columbo #1]

"Well, you don't believe in Zeus or Apollo or hundreds of other gods, right?"

"Right. I believe in one God, the God of the Bible."

"So, I just believe in one less god than you do."

"Right. I agree. Why is that significant?"

"Well, that means we're almost the same. You're basically an atheist."

"So, do you think I'm basically a bachelor?"

"Of course not. You're married."

"Well, there are billions of women I'm not married to, and a bachelor has only one less wife than I do."

"That makes no sense."

"I agree."

4. Both atheists and Christians make claims. Intellectual integrity requires that both give reasons for their views. We're ready to do that.

Providing that positive evidence for God is our next step in responding to atheism on the street.

IV. God, the Best Explanation

A. **Annabeth's question:**
   1. When my daughter was eight years old, she asked, "How do we know God is true?"
   2. Here's the simplest way I've found to explain why theism is a more defensible option than atheism: *God is the best explanation for the way things are.*
      a. God's existence makes sense of features of the world that, without him, would be unlikely in the extreme.
      b. Atheism, on the other hand, explains nothing. It is the ultimate non-explanation, "explaining" by denying that explanations exist.

> **Ambassador Skills**
>
> Note the advantage of this "best explanation" strategy. There's no need to dismiss the *possibility* of other options. We are free to consider alternatives. We're not dogmatically insisting that ours is the *only* explanation, just the one we think is the *best* explanation, all things considered.

Here are two applications of this "best explanation" principle:

B. **Beginning at the beginning**
   1. I was once asked during an audience Q&A to give some compelling evidence for the existence of God. In Columbo style, I made my case by asking three simple questions:

a. Do things exist? Yes, they do.
b. Have they always existed? No, the universe came into existence at some time in the distant past.[11]
c. What caused the universe to come into existence? There are only two choices:
    (1) Some thing caused the universe to come into existence or . . .
    (2) No thing caused the universe to come into existence.[12]

Reflect a Moment

At this point, the skeptic who leans on reason finds himself in a box. Both the law of excluded middle (it can't be neither option because there's no third choice) and the law of noncontradiction (it can't be both since that's a contradiction) oblige him to choose one of the only two logical possibilities.

d. Who is in his rational rights to say, "Nothing caused the world"?
    (1) Even if it's *possible* that something could come from nothing—something that's unlikely in the extreme—what is most *reasonable*?
    (2) For example, is this dialogue believable?

> **WIFE:** "Where did that Mercedes SL in our garage come from?"
> **HUSBAND:** "It just popped into existence out of nothing, honey. That's the way the whole universe started, so I don't know why it can't happen to a little Mercedes."

    (3) The something-from-nothing option is worse than magic.
        (a) In magic, a magician pulls a rabbit out of a hat.
        (b) In this case, there's no magician and there's no hat—just a rabbit (the universe) appearing out of nowhere.

---

11. For an accounting of the prodigious scientific evidence for an absolute beginning of the universe, see Stephen C. Meyer, *Return of the God Hypothesis* (New York: HarperCollins, 2021), chs. 4–6.
12. I say "no thing" instead of "nothing" because some treat "nothing" like a kind of something. Odd, but it happens. Substituting "no thing" avoids that liability.

2. This kind of argument is called a *cosmological* argument—an argument for the existence of God based on the existence of the cosmos, the universe.
3. Let me put it simply and directly: a big bang needs a big banger.[13] That pretty much covers it.
4. Skeptics know this, too.
   a. Once, at a dinner party, a young man sitting across from me announced—somewhat belligerently—that he no longer believed in God. "It's irrational," he said. "There's no evidence."
      (1) I asked him if he thought the big bang banged itself, but he dismissed my question.
      (2) I then asked that if he heard a knock on the front door across the room, would he think the knock knocked itself, or would he conclude that someone was knocking on the door? Again, he dismissed my point.
      (3) Ironically, twenty minutes later there was a loud knock on the front door (I'm not making this up). He lifted his head and said, "Who's that?" I said, "Nobody." Nevertheless, he got up and answered the door.
      (4) Even the atheist knew a simple knock couldn't knock itself. Yet he seemed completely willing to accept that an entire universe just popped into existence without rhyme, reason, or purpose.
   b. No, atheism cannot explain where the world came from. Theism can. Thus, theism is the best explanation for the way things are—the existence of the universe, in this case.
5. At this point, you might get pushback: "Who created God?"
   a. Richard Dawkins thinks theism has "utterly failed" because apparently there's no answer to a question he says even children know to ask.
      (1) Kids ask, "Who created God?" because they're kids.
      (2) Grown-ups ought to know better.
         (a) The question "Who created . . . whatever?" only applies to things that *begin* to exist.

---

13. I realize the big bang is controversial for many Christians because the event is generally associated with an ancient universe. The critical detail here, though, is that modern science, despite its biases, affirms a de facto creation event that fits nicely with our own story but is a mystery with materialism. Even Christians who are not convinced of the big bang can still leverage the skeptic's belief in their own favor.

(b) Yet no one in this discussion—even atheists—believes that if God existed he'd be the kind of being that needed a beginning.
6. Here's how I would approach this issue in conversation:

"Who created God?"

"Let me ask you a question. What are you assuming when you ask, 'Who *created* God?'"

"Well, I guess I'm assuming God was created."

"Exactly. So why would you think that if there is a God, he'd need to be created?"

"Well, you think the universe was created."

"I do, because the universe had a beginning—which you believe, too, right?"

"Right."

"So, if God existed, why would you think a self-existent Being like him would need to be created? Wouldn't that be a contradiction?"

7. Here's the point:
   a. No matter what view of reality you take—a religious view or a nonreligious one—there must be an *ultimate* starting point for everything. If not, you're stuck with an infinite regress of causes that never allows you to get to a beginning ("Who made that?" "Okay, but who made *that*?" and so on, *ad infinitum*).
   b. The material universe can't be the ultimate starting point because we know it came into existence sometime in the distant past.
      (1) It must be something outside the natural realm.
      (2) It also must be something that can start the process by deciding to cause everything else to come into being.
   c. In other words, the ultimate starting point must be some *one*, not some *thing*. That's why it makes no sense to ask, "Who created God?"[14]

---

14. I go into more detail on the problem with the question "Who created God?" in *The Story of Reality* (Grand Rapids: Zondervan, 2017), 50–51.

So, theism does a better job of explaining the existence of the universe than atheism does. It explains something else better, too.

C. Making contact
1. Let me introduce my second evidence with a question: How would we know if there's intelligent life in other parts of the universe? Scientists know the answer.
    a. We'd know if we discover something coming from another world that couldn't have been produced by natural causes.
    b. That's the basis for the scientific project known as SETI, the Search for Extraterrestrial Intelligence.
2. SETI's basic way of recognizing intelligent life beyond Earth was featured years back in a fascinating movie called *Contact*.
    a. In the movie, SETI astronomer Ellie Arroway (Jodie Foster) decodes a message from radio signals from outer space. Embedded in the signal is a detailed blueprint of instructions to build a spaceship. The blueprint completely convinces Ellie that aliens exist.
    b. Curiously, though, Ellie is not convinced about God's existence. She needs evidence, she says.
    c. Yet if Ellie applied the same criterion to the question of God that she applied to the question of E.T.s, she would have had the evidence she needed.
        (1) The evidence for the existence of God is exactly the same kind of evidence Ellie took as proof for the existence of aliens: a sophisticated blueprint.
        (2) Every single cell in her body carried in it a code—embedded in her DNA—of a detailed blueprint far more complex than the one she discovered for the spaceship.
3. In our computer age, we know where code comes from.
    a. Code comes from programmers. It's designed by intelligence.
    b. So, here's the question:
        (1) Who wrote the DNA code in each one of our bodies?
        (2) Who combined three billion base pair "words" to write the assembly instructions for human beings?

D. Fingerprints everywhere

1. And DNA is just the tip of the design iceberg. Signs of intelligence—God's fingerprints—are everywhere in the natural world.
2. Richard Dawkins opens his bestselling book *The Blind Watchmaker* with these words: "Biology is the study of complicated things that give the appearance of having been designed for a purpose."[15]
3. Of course, Dawkins doesn't think biological life was intelligently designed. He's convinced the "blind watchmaker" of evolution did the designing.
   a. But think about this:
      (1) There's the stunning ability of reptiles (sea turtles), fish (salmon), mammals (whales), and insects (monarch butterflies) to navigate to precise locations on the globe using some type of internal GPS.
      (2) It's unthinkable that the same incredibly sophisticated system could evolve by accident independently in creatures so far removed from one another on the alleged evolutionary tree of life.[16]
   b. In our solar system, there's the remarkable positioning of planet Earth in just the right place in our planetary system and with just the right qualities to make life possible—what even secular scientists call the "Goldilocks Zone."
      (1) Just the right size
      (2) Just the right seasons dictated by just the right tilt of Earth's axis
      (3) Just the right magnetic field with just the right intensity
      (4) Just the right moon creating just the right tides and just the right continental drift
      (5) Just the right ratio of oxygen to nitrogen
      (6) Just the right ratio of carbon dioxide to water vapor. And on and on and on.
   c. Without this "just right" fine-tuning, intelligent life on planet Earth would not be possible.
4. This kind of argument is called a *teleological* or design argument—an argument for the existence of God based on evidence for design in the universe.

---

15. Richard Dawkins, *The Blind Watchmaker* (New York: Norton, 1986), 1.
16. See the superb Illustra Media DVDs *Living Waters* and *Metamorphosis* for details. Their *Flight* DVD is also stunning.

🗨 Reflect a Moment

These remarkable features (and there are many more examples) are so stunning given naturalism, they prompted astrophysicist Sir Fred Hoyle—who originally coined the term *big bang*—to admit, "A commonsense interpretation of the facts suggests that a superintellect has monkeyed with physics, as well as with chemistry and biology, and that there are no blind forces worth speaking about in nature. The numbers one calculates from the facts seem to me so overwhelming as to put this conclusion almost beyond question."[17]

5. Clearly, God's "fingerprints" are everywhere for those willing to look. There are lots of ways to make this point in conversation. Here's one example:

   "There's no evidence for God."

   "Let me ask you a question. If you saw a shoe print in the sand on the beach, what would you conclude?"

   "Someone had been walking there."

   "Right, a person wearing shoes."

   "Right."

   "Would you be tempted to think it was a freak accident of nature—seashells, sand, and surf all rolling around together, creating an impression that looked like a shoe print but wasn't?"

   "That wouldn't make any sense."

   "Why not?"

   "Because first, chance can't produce a shoe print, and second, there's a better explanation: a person wearing a shoe."

   "Exactly. Now another example. Let's say you found a blueprint of some sort. Would you be tempted to think it was a crazy accident of ink spilled on paper and tossed around by natural forces?"

   "Of course not, for the same reasons."

   "So, what do you make of the human body?"

   "It evolved by chance."

---

17. Fred Hoyle, "The Universe: Past and Present Reflection," *Annual Review of Astronomy and Astrophysics* 20 (1982): 16.

"And the DNA blueprint for the human body inside each one of our cells?"

"It evolved by chance."

"Why would you believe a human body evolved by chance, when you can't believe a simple shoe print in the sand happened by chance?"

"Well, it's possible."

"Let's say I agreed. Even if it were possible—which strikes me as unlikely—do you think it's the most *reasonable* option? Is it the odds-on favorite? Plus, there's a better explanation."

"What?"

"An intelligent creator."

6. So, to answer Richard Dawkins, maybe living things—and the rest of the universe, for that matter—"appear" to be designed because they *are* designed. Maybe, all things considered, God actually is the best explanation for the way things are.

E. **I have given two good reasons to believe that God is the best explanation for the way things are:**
   1. One: the origin of the universe—the cosmological argument
   2. Two: the dazzling design at every level of our world—the teleological argument
   3. Both point to God and not to atheism as the best explanation for the way the world is.

V. What Main Points Did We Cover in This Session?

A. **First, I explained why the God question is the most important question anyone can answer.**
   1. The answer you give to that one question sets the course for everything that follows.
   2. All the big questions eventually come down to the answer to one question:
      a. Are we our own, and therefore we are in charge?
      b. Or do we belong to Someone else, and therefore he is in charge?

SESSION 4

B. **Second, I talked about four different distractions atheists offer that can throw you off track.**
   1. They redefine atheism as lacking belief in God.
   2. They redefine faith as belief without evidence.
   3. They say belief in God is irrational.
   4. They imply that Christians are mostly atheists because they deny all other gods but one.

C. **Third, I gave you two powerful evidences that the smart money is on theism, not on atheism, as the best explanation for the way things are.**
   1. One, a cosmological argument for God based on the origin of the universe—a big bang needs a big banger.
   2. Two, a teleological argument based on powerful evidence for design in the DNA blueprint, design in the biological world, and design in the solar system

D. **I also answered the challenge "Who created God?"**
   1. I pointed out that every worldview must start somewhere with some kind of uncaused cause.
   2. I showed why God is the best candidate for that starting point, given the evidence.

? Self-Assessment

Try to answer the following questions without using your notes.

1. Why is God's existence the structural starting point for everything else in life?
   ➤ God's existence is the structural starting point because all the big _____ come down to one _____: Who is in _____? Either _____ is or man is.

2. How do atheists now redefine atheism?
   ➤ Atheists now say they merely _____ belief in God.

3. Why is this move a misleading misstep?
   ➤ Atheists may lack a belief *in* God, but they do not lack a belief _____ God.

4. List the three possible responses to the claim that God exists.
   ➤ You can _____ it ("God does exist"), you can _____ it ("God does not exist"), or you can withhold judgment ("I'm _____").

5. How do atheists redefine faith?
   ➤ *Faith* is the word people use when they have no good _____ or _____ to justify their beliefs.

6. What is the biblical view of faith?
   ➤ According to Scripture, faith is active _____ in what we have good _____ to believe is true. The Bible never promotes _____ faith or a _____ of faith.

7. When someone says, "It's irrational to believe in God," what is the first question you ask?
   ➤ The first question is "Precisely what is _____ about belief in God?"

8. What question do you ask if an atheist says there is no good evidence for God?
   ➤ You ask, "What specific _____ or _____ for God have you thought about or _____?"

9. What is the simplest way to explain why theism is a more defensible option than atheism?
   ➤ God is the best _____ for the way things are.

10. What is the name for the argument for God based on the existence of the universe?
    ➤ The argument for God based on the existence of the universe is called the _____ argument.

11. What is a simple way of stating one form of that argument?
    ➤ A big _____ needs a big _____.

12. What is being assumed with the question, "Who created God?"
    ➤ The question assumes that God was _____.

13. Give two reasons that is an unreasonable assumption.
    > One, the God we're talking about is self-_____, so he needs no _____. Two, no matter what view of reality one takes, there must be an _____ starting point for everything to avoid an _____ regress of causes that never allows us to get to a beginning.

14. What is the name for the argument for God based on evidence from design in the universe?
    > The argument for God based on evidence from design in the universe is called the _____ argument.

15. Name one powerful evidence for design based on biology.
    > Powerful evidence for design based on biology is the complex _____ found in our _____. It is basically a _____ giving detailed plans or instructions for our biological development.

16. Name one powerful evidence for design based on the astronomy of our solar system. What do secular scientists call this phenomenon?
    > Earth is finely _____ and _____ just right for intelligent life to be possible on our planet. Secular scientists call this phenomenon the "_____ Zone."

☑ **Self-Assessment with Answers**

1. God's existence is the structural starting point because all the big **questions** come down to one **question**: Who is in **charge**? Either **God** is or man is.
2. Atheists now say they merely **lack** belief in God.
3. Atheists may lack a belief *in* God, but they do not lack a belief *about* God.
4. You can **affirm** it ("God does exist"), you can **deny** it ("God does not exist"), or you can withhold judgment ("I'm **neutral**").
5. *Faith* is the word people use when they have no good **reasons** or **evidence** to justify their beliefs.
6. According to Scripture, faith is active **trust** in what we have good **reason** to believe is true. The Bible never promotes **blind** faith or a **leap** of faith.

7. The first question is "Precisely what is **irrational** about belief in God?"
8. You ask, "What specific **arguments** or **evidence** for God have you thought about or **considered**?"
9. God is the best **explanation** for the way things are.
10. The argument for God based on the existence of the universe is called the **cosmological** argument.
11. A big **bang** needs a big **banger**.
12. The question assumes that God was **created**.
13. One, the God we're talking about is self-**existent**, so he needs no **beginning**. Two, no matter what view of reality one takes, there must be an **ultimate** starting point for everything to avoid an **infinite** regress of causes that never allows us to get to a beginning.
14. The argument for God based on evidence from design in the universe is called the **teleological** argument.
15. Powerful evidence for design based on biology is the complex **code** found in our **DNA**. It is basically a **blueprint** giving detailed plans or instructions for our biological development.
16. Earth is finally **tuned** and **positioned** just right for intelligent life to be possible on our planet. Secular scientists call this phenomenon the "**Goldilocks** Zone."

Interactive Group Study Questions

1. Why is the existence of God the most decisive issue in life? Discuss how the big questions and the secondary questions are affected by our answer to the question "Are we our own, or do we belong to Someone else?"
2. What is the first distraction Greg talks about that is often raised by an atheist? Explain how you might use the first Columbo question to deal with this distraction.
3. Many atheists try to define *faith* in a way that keeps Christians from defending their view. Talk about how redefining faith as the opposite of having evidence does not represent the Christian view. What does the term *straw man* mean, and how does it apply here?
4. Biblical faith means active trust based on reasons and evidence. What are some examples of this kind of faith in Scripture?

5. Sometimes an atheist might claim that belief in God is irrational because "there is no evidence." How would you respond to this claim?
6. Name two examples Greg gives of his "best explanation" principle for assessing worldviews. Discuss other examples you have used in your own conversations with others.
7. Discuss why the question "Who created God?" is not appropriate for theists.

Going Deeper: Information for Self-Study

Explain to a friend the things you learned in this lesson.

1. Go over the four distractions atheists often offer and your responses to them.
2. Then explain as best you can two of the significant evidences for God's existence.
3. Also explain why the "Who made God?" question doesn't really make any sense.
4. Be prepared to share your experiences with the group when you get together next time.

Food for Thought

Knowledge versus Belief

Atheists sometimes call themselves agnostics because, they say, they don't *know for sure* that God doesn't exist. This is confused terminology. *Theist*, *atheist*, and *agnostic* are not words that describe *knowledge* categories, but rather words that describe *beliefs* (ergo "believer" versus "nonbeliever"). Most of our beliefs are fallible (capable of being false). We still *believe* they're true, though—often with good reason—even if we don't *know* for sure.

If agnosticism means lack of complete certainty, then each of us is agnostic on just about everything we think we know. Atheists aren't agnostics. Rather, they're believers of a certain stripe. They believe that God does not exist.

Reality Our Friend

Our confidence in Christianity is based on a powerful concept: *reality is on our side*. God's existence makes sense of features of the world that without him would be unlikely in the extreme. Other worldview stories do not fare well by this standard because obvious details of the world simply do not fit into their narrative, putting them on a collision course with reality.[18]

See, Hear, Touch, Behold

In 1 John the beloved disciple implicitly clarifies the biblical view of faith. He opens his letter with the evidence of his own eyewitness encounter with Christ. Notice how many senses he appeals to:

> What was from the beginning, what we have *heard*, what we have *seen with our eyes*, what we have *looked at* and *touched with our hands*, concerning the Word of Life—and the life was manifested, and we have *seen* and testify and proclaim to you the eternal life, which was with the Father and was manifested to us—what we have *seen and heard* we proclaim to you also. (1 John 1:1–3, emphasis added)

He closes his letter this way:

> And the testimony is this, that God has given us eternal life, and this life is in His Son. He who has the Son has the life; he who does not have the Son of God does not have the life. These things I have written to you who believe in the name of the Son of God, so that you may *know* that you have eternal life. (1 John 5:11–13, emphasis added)

To John, faith wasn't a blind leap. It wasn't wishing on a star. It was grounded in evidence that led to knowledge. And when the evidence is so overwhelming—as it was for the earliest followers of Jesus (and many since then)—the knowledge is certain.

"Who Created God, Daddy?"

If one of your children asks, "Who created God, Daddy?" you might amend your dialogue this way: "If I asked you, 'Are you still cheating on your tests in school?' what would I be assuming?" Let them chew on it for a bit until they get the right answer about their tests—maybe with a little help from you.

---

18. See, e.g., Nancy Pearcey, *Finding Truth: 5 Principles for Unmasking Atheism, Secularism, and Other God Substitutes* (Colorado Springs, CO: Cook, 2015).

Next, ask them, "Okay, since your question assumes that God was created, what makes you think that's what happened? Is that what the Bible teaches? [Interaction] No, the Bible teaches that God is eternal. Do you know what that means? [Interaction] It means God never had a beginning, and he will never have an end. Do you see that it doesn't really make sense, then, to ask the question about the beginning of God if he had no beginning?"

You get the idea. Pursue a conversation with them in which you tease out these concepts with questions. I think they'll catch on quickly.

SESSION 5

EVIL: ATHEISM'S FATAL FLAW

Demonstrating Mastery

Try recalling the answers to the following questions without using your notes. The answers are in the "Self-Assessment with Answers" section of session 4.

1. When someone says, "It's irrational to believe in God," what is the first question you ask?
2. What question do you ask if an atheist says there is no good evidence for God?
3. What is the simplest way to explain why theism is a more defensible option than atheism?
4. What is the name for the argument for God based on the existence of the universe? What is a simple way of stating one form of that argument?
5. Name one powerful evidence for design based on the astronomy of our solar system. What do secular scientists call this phenomenon?

I. Review and Looking Ahead

A. In the preceding session, we covered the following:
1. First, I explained why the God question is the most important question anyone can answer.

      a. The answer you give to that one question sets the course for everything that follows.

      b. All the big questions eventually come down to the answer to one question: "Are we our own, or do we belong to Someone else?"

2. Second, I talked about four different distractions atheists offer that can throw you off track.

      a. They redefine atheism as lacking belief in God.

      b. They redefine faith as belief without evidence.

      c. They say belief in God is irrational.

      d. They imply that Christians are mostly atheists because they deny all other gods but one.

3. Third, I gave you two powerful evidences that the smart money is on theism, not on atheism, as the best explanation for the way things are.

      a. One, a cosmological argument for God based on the origin of the universe—a big bang needs a big banger.

      b. Two, a design argument based on powerful evidence for design in the DNA blueprint, in the biological world, and in astronomy.

4. I also answered the challenge "Who created God?"

      a. I pointed out that every worldview must start somewhere with some kind of uncaused cause.

      b. I showed why God is the best candidate for that starting point, given the evidence.

B. Here is what we'll cover in this session:

1. First, I'll make my final application of our "best explanation" principle against atheism by showing you how the problem of evil is evidence *for* God, not *against* him.

2. Second, I'll show that if relativism is true, then it's impossible for there to be a problem of evil.

3. Finally, I'll explain why Darwinian evolution is not an alternative to God as a way of accounting for objective morality.

II. Evil: Atheism's Fatal Flaw

A. The problem of evil is for many people one of the most persuasive challenges to the existence of God.

1. You know the reasoning:

    a. A good God would *want* to get rid of all evil.

    b. A powerful God would *be able* to get rid of all evil.

    c. Yet evil remains. Therefore, there is no God.

2. This challenge is called the "deductive problem of evil," and it fails.[1]

    a. In a word, the charge does not stand up since it's certainly conceivable that a good, powerful God might allow evil *if he had good reason to do so.*

    b. This mere possibility is enough to nullify the contradiction, which is why philosophers rarely raise this version of the problem of evil anymore.[2]

▎ Reflect a Moment

The atheist's rejection of God because of the problem of evil solves nothing. As I have written elsewhere, "Removing God from the equation, though understandable, does nothing to eliminate the problem that caused someone to doubt God's existence in the first place. God is gone, but the original problem remains. The world is still broken. Atheism settles nothing on this matter. . . . Things still are not the way they're supposed to be, so the atheist continues to be plagued with the same problem he started with."[3]

B. I want you to see a different problem with this challenge, though.

1. Evil not only fails to disprove God. It is actually evidence for God and against atheism.

---

1. See Gregory Koukl, *The Story of Reality* (Grand Rapids: Zondervan, 2017), ch. 14; and Gregory Ganssle, "God and Evil," part 3 in *Thinking about God: First Steps in Philosophy* (Downers Grove, IL: InterVarsity, 2004).

2. A variation known as the *inductive problem of evil* is still in play. Regardless, since both the deductive and the inductive complaint rely on the existence of *genuine* evil—objective evil—they both falter for the same reason I'm arguing here. Thus, my approach dispatches both birds with the same stone.

3. Koukl, *Story of Reality*, 35.

2. In fact, I think the problem of evil is atheism's fatal flaw. Here is the key strategic move:
   a. We're not going to try to answer why a good, powerful God allowed evil—a hard question to answer since God didn't tell us.
   b. Rather, we're going to show that God must exist for there to be a problem of evil in the first place.

🚩 Reflect a Moment

Thoughtful attempts at explaining why God allowed evil in the first place are called *theodicies*. Most have merit, but they are somewhat speculative since God has not revealed his mind on this issue.

C. Our strategy trades on two facts that are—surprisingly—embedded in the objection itself.
   1. First fact: the problem of evil is real, and everyone knows it.
      a. Every thoughtful person, no matter where he lives or when he lived, knows something is terribly wrong with the world.
      b. Things are not the way they're supposed to be.
   2. Second fact: the evil that people are concerned with is objective evil, evil "in the world."
      a. When people identify the bad stuff . . .
         (1) They aren't simply saying they don't *like* what's happening.
         (2) They're not saying they personally *prefer* things to be different. That's relativism.
      b. They're convinced some things happen that are deeply wrong in themselves, even if other people disagree.
      c. They believe the actions or events are objectively evil, even if they don't use those precise words.

D. Real evil requires that morality be objective, not subjective.
   1. The evil is on the *outside*, out there in the world.
   2. It's not simply something a person dislikes on the *inside*.

a. If morality is relative, if it's only a matter of human opinion on the inside . .
   b. Then there is no real evil on the outside—in the world—and the objection to God based on evil vanishes.
 3. Since everyone knows that evil is real, then everyone—even atheists—implicitly affirm objective morality.

Here's another way of looking at that same point:

 4. In order to have broken laws, you must first have had laws.
   a. Can you break the speed limit on Germany's famous autobahn?
      (1) No. Why? Because there is no speed limit.
      (2) You can't break a law that doesn't exist.
   b. According to relativism, there are no moral laws governing the world, so no moral laws can be broken, and thus there can't be a problem of evil in the world. Let that sink in.

Here's our final step:

E. You can't have transcendent laws that are broken, causing the problem of evil, if you do not have a transcendent lawmaker.
 1. That would be God.
 2. If there is no lawmaker, there are no laws. Let that sink in, too.

Reflect a Moment

Put in a playful way, it makes no sense to say things are *not* the way they're s'posed to be (the problem of evil) unless there *is* a way they're s'posed to be. And there can't *be* a way they're s'posed to be without a "S'poser." Translation: it's going to be difficult to make sense of transcendent moral law without a transcendent moral lawgiver—God.

F. Why believe in God?
 1. *Because* of the problem of evil, not in *spite* of it.

2. The existence of God is the best explanation for our deeply embedded understanding that the world is not the way it's supposed to be.

3. Of course, this doesn't explain *why* God allowed evil, but strategically in conversations that's not our project. We simply want to show that evil is evidence *for* God, not *against* him.

G. This line of reasoning is called the *moral argument* for God. Put formally:

1. If there is no God—no lawmaker—there is no objective morality—no laws.

2. But there is objective morality. We know this because of the problem of evil.

3. Therefore, there is a God.[4] God is the best explanation—even for the problem of evil.[5]

III. Evil in the Street

So, in conversations, how do we capitalize on this insight? With questions, of course.

A. My standard opening question when someone raises the problem of evil is this: "What exactly is the problem as you see it?" (Columbo #1).

1. This question accomplishes two things.

    a. First, it buys me time—maybe only a moment or two—so I can collect my thoughts and think about my next moves.

    b. Second, I want my challenger to spell out his concern in precise terms.

    (1) That helps him get clear on his own complaint.

    (2) It also eliminates ambiguities for both of us.

2. Here's how the conversation might flow from there:

    "So, you believe in evil, then?"[6]

---

4. This syllogism is a logically valid form of argument called *modus tollens*.

5. For a more thorough discussion of why citing evil in favor of atheism is self-defeating, see Greg Koukl, "Evil as Evidence for God," Stand to Reason, February 5, 2013, www.str.org/w/evil-as-evidence-for-god.

6. Notice, by the way, my persistent use of clarification questions (Columbo #1) both to confirm important information and to keep the conversation moving forward in a friendly, interactive way.

"Right. That's why I don't believe in God."

"Let's just say you're right, and God doesn't exist. All those things you described as bad and evil those things still happen, right?"

"Of course they do."

"And those things are still evil, right?"

"Of course."

"That's a bit confusing, isn't it?"

"Why?"

"Well, how do you, as an atheist, explain those evils in the world?"

"I don't follow." [Be prepared for people to be confused here.]

"You asked me how a good, powerful God could exist when there's so much evil in the world."

"Right."

"Now I'm asking, if atheism—your view—is true, how can there be so much evil in the world?"

"I still don't get it."

"Okay, let me put it this way. When you say things happen that are evil, where are you getting your standard to judge things as evil in themselves?"

"It's just common sense."

"Right, but now you're saying how you *know* evil. I'm asking a different question. You may know what the speed limit is by looking at the signs, but where do speed limits come from to begin with?"

"The government, of course."

"Exactly. So, what governing authority over the whole world sets the limits that get broken, resulting in the evil you're concerned about? That's my question."

3. Here's a second way of making the same point:

"So, you believe in evil, then?"

"Yes, of course."

"You're an atheist, though, so I don't understand your concern."

"What do you mean?"

"If there is no God, how can there be the kind of real evil in the world that you're concerned about?" [Columbo #3]

"I don't get your point."

"Well, when you talk about evil, you're basically saying some kind of moral rule has been broken, that the person doing evil has broken that rule. Right?"

"I guess so."

"Then who made those rules?" [Columbo #3]

B. If a person wants to reject God yet still wants to hang on to morality . . .

1. He has to offer an alternative that's able to explain real, objective morality in a universe without God as the lawmaker.
2. The main contender is Darwinism, so let's talk a bit about that option.

IV. Good without God?

A. Until recently, atheists have generally agreed that if there is no God, there is no real morality.

1. Times have changed, though. You might have seen billboards that read:
    a. "No God? No problem. Be good for goodness' sake."
    b. "Are you good without God? Millions are."
    c. The point is clear:
        (1) Morality does not depend on belief in God.
        (2) Atheists can be good, too.
2. Atheist Christopher Hitchens often challenged his religious opponents to name a single act of goodness a theist could do that an atheist couldn't do.

▶ Reflect a Moment

Careful theists do not claim that *belief* in God is necessary to *do* good, but rather that *God* is necessary for any act *to be* good in the first place, that without him true morality has no foundation at all. The question is not whether believers and nonbelievers can perform the same *behaviors*—of course they can—but whether any behavior can be good in a materialistic world bereft of God.

B. Remember, objective morality is the issue here.
1. Our argument is that only objective morality can make sense of the problem of evil, and transcendent moral obligations require a transcendent source.
2. Atheists disagree. The first premise of our moral argument for God ("If there is no God, there is no objective morality") is false, they say.
    a. God is not necessary for goodness.
    b. Darwinism can do the job all on its own.
        (1) Morality helps us as a species—the argument goes—to get our genes into the next generation.
        (2) Nature selects the survivors. Moral genes win. Simple.
3. Can evolution explain ethics?
    a. Can "goodness" and "badness" be reduced to biology?
    b. Can Mother Nature—mixing genetic mutation with natural selection—supplant Father God as morality's maker?
4. Do not forget—and this is key—only *objective* morality can make sense of real evil in the world.
    a. If morality is relative—just a matter of personal preference and not something that is actually wrong or wicked in itself . . .
    b. Then there is no evil *in the world*, and therefore there is no problem of evil
5. Here's the question: Is Darwinian evolution capable of producing the kind of morality necessary to make sense of the problem of evil?

Let's see . . .

C. Answering Hitchens's challenge reveals the serious problem for the Darwinian alternative.

1. Hitchens asked the theist to name a single act of goodness the theist can perform that Hitchens the atheist couldn't do. His challenge completely misses the point, though.
    a. It does not matter if an atheist can do all the same *actions* that theists call good. Any atheist can perform the same *behaviors*—no question.
        (1) He can feed the poor. He can love his neighbor.
        (2) He can even sacrifice his life for others.
    b. The issue is whether those behaviors can be genuinely objectively *good* if there is no God.
2. Think for a moment about the relationship of writers to readers.
    a. If I handed a copy of Mark Twain's *Tom Sawyer* to you, could you read it? Of course you could.
    b. What if you said, though, that Mark Twain never existed? What if you said that you didn't believe *any* writer existed? Could you still read *Tom Sawyer* if I handed a copy to you? Sure you could.
    c. If you were right that there were no writers, though, there'd be nothing to read in the first place. The fact that you have a book to read is evidence that there was a writer who wrote it.

▶ Reflect a Moment

Readers who deny authors sound silly. Sure, they wouldn't need to *believe* in authors to be good readers. They could challenge you to show them one article you could read as a believer (in writers) that they couldn't read as unbelievers, and you'd be hard-pressed. Yet their retort would not rescue them from their foolishness. Articles are, by nature, the kinds of things that require authors.

3. Objective morality is just the same.
    a. Morality is evidence for God the same way books are evidence for authors.
    b. The issue is not whether one can act according to a moral code or not, but whether we can account for the code to begin with.

c. When atheists say they can be moral without God, it's like saying they can be law-abiding citizens in a land without laws.

   (1) *Belief* in God isn't necessary to do the behavior.

   (2) Rather, *God* is necessary for any behavior to be good—genuinely good—in the first place.

▶ Reflect a Moment

Hitchens was wrong on another point. As an atheist, he *couldn't* do all the good things a theist can do. He could never do the *summum bonum*, the greatest good. He could never love God with his whole heart, mind, soul, and strength. He could not worship the one from whom all goodness comes. Of course, Hitchens would likely sniff at this point, but we mustn't miss the deeper implication. Regardless of who is right on the God question, the entire moral project is altered significantly when God is added to the equation. Simply put, the atheist and the theist do not share the same morality.

D. It's impossible for Darwinism to explain the only kind of morality able to make sense of the problem of evil—objective morality.

1. How does evolution allegedly work to create morality?

   a. Simply put, natural selection chooses among genetic mutations, selecting those traits that are best suited for survival and reproduction.

   b. Morality improves our chances of reproducing. Therefore, evolution can account for morality.

2. As a side note . . .

   a. The Darwinian option is only a theoretical explanation of how an evolutionary process *might* produce moral beliefs in humans.

   b. Offering that as a possibility, though, is not the same as actually *showing* that natural selection working on genetic mutations has produced our moral convictions.

      (1) Precisely how does a merely biological process produce beliefs?

      (2) How can reshuffling molecules cause immaterial beliefs about morality to spontaneously spring into existence?

3. Nevertheless, I want to show you that . . .

a. Even if Darwinism were able to produce beliefs . . .

b. Even if "good" and "bad" were genetically transferable, physical traits . . .

c. Darwinian evolution still could not account for *objective* morality.

E. I want you to think very carefully about the Darwinian account of morality.

1. Atheists want to undermine the moral argument for God by invoking evolution.

2. To do this, though, they have to explain how a purely naturalistic process produces *objective* morality. Relativism won't do.

    a. Remember, relativism is mind dependent. It's based on beliefs *inside* a person.

    b. Objective morality, though, is mind independent. It's based on facts *outside* the person.

3. So here's my question:

    a. What is the only kind of morality Darwinism can give us, even in principle?

    b. Can biology make anything in the world—outside a person—truly bad? Of course not. Molecules can't make murder wrong.

    c. Biology can only make a person *believe on the inside* that something is bad because that belief provides some evolutionary benefit. That is relativism.

4. Atheist philosopher and Darwinist Michael Ruse is crystal clear on this point:

    a. "We are genetically determined to believe that we ought to help each other."[7] "Ultimately," he says, "morality is an illusion put in place by our genes."[8]

    b. He's right, too, if evolution accounts for morality.

        (1) Evolutionary morality is simply a *subjective* illusion.

        (2) Darwinism cannot create *objective* morality.

5. So, even if evolution can explain our *sense* of morality (though I'm skeptical), nevertheless . . .

    a. It can only produce subjective, relativistic morality. And relativism is not enough to make sense of the problem of evil.

    b. The moral argument for God—that without God there can be no objective morality—still goes through. Evolution can't touch it.

---

7. R. Keith Loftin, ed. *God and Morality—Four Views* (Downers Grove, IL: InterVarsity, 2012), 60.
8. Ibid., 69.

6. Here's how you might make this point in conversation:

"Do you mind if I ask you a few questions to get clear on your view?"
"Go ahead."
"I've been saying that if there really is a problem of evil, then God must exist to provide the standard for good and bad. You disagree."
"Right."
"You believe in morality, but as an atheist, you think there's no need for God. Darwinism can explain right and wrong. Correct?" [Columbo #1]
"Correct."
"Can you help me understand exactly how that works?" [a request for further clarification]
"Well, mutations produce changes that cause feelings about things like altruism or kindness that nature selects to help the group survive. Standard stuff."
"Right. So, strictly speaking, to say something is 'good' or 'bad' is just another way of saying natural selection makes us feel a certain way about some behavior, so we label it 'right' or 'wrong.' Is that correct?"
"Pretty much."
"So, if I understand correctly, the idea of good and evil is completely inside the person who evolved that way. If we'd evolved differently, we might have had completely different ideas of what was right or wrong. Correct?" [Columbo #1]
"Yep. Just like with our physical bodies. With different mutations, humans could have evolved bodies that looked much different from the ones we have now."
"Got it. Would you say, then, that this kind of morality is centered 'inside'—so to speak—the person who evolved that way? It's their internal beliefs or feelings?"
"Exactly. Like you said, if we'd evolved differently, we'd have different beliefs about right or wrong."
"That's what confuses me. If morality is simply beliefs or feelings inside a person because he evolved that way, that's just another form of relativism, right?"

"I guess so."

"Do you see the problem that is for you?"

"Not really, no."

"Well, earlier you raised the problem of evil in the world—objective evil. I said that requires God. But you said no, evolution can explain that. But then you explained how evolution causes subjective, relativistic morality, not objective morality. So, how does evolutionary relativistic morality help us understand why there's real, objective evil in the world?"

V. What Main Points Did We Cover in This Session?

A. First, I showed you how, if relativism is true, it's impossible for there to be a problem of evil.
1. Real evil happens when real objective moral laws are broken.
2. If there are no objective moral laws, then there can't be any broken laws.
3. If there aren't any broken moral laws, then there is no problem of evil.

B. Second, I showed you how the problem of evil is actually evidence *for* God, not *against* him.
1. Real moral laws—laws that transcend mere human opinion—have to be broken in the world for there to be a real problem of evil.
2. But you can't have transcendent laws that are broken, causing the problem of evil, if you don't have a transcendent lawmaker. That would be God.

C. Finally, we looked at an alternative explanation offered for the existence of morality: Darwinian evolution.
1. First, we learned that even though atheists can mimic the behavior of theists, if God didn't exist, then no behavior—by atheists or theists—could be objectively good or bad.
    a. Just as writers are necessary for books to exist . . .
    b. God is necessary for real goodness to exist.

2. Second, I pointed out that morality without God simply is not the same as morality with God since honoring God is the greatest good in Christian morality. Atheists can't do that.
3. Third, we learned that even if evolution were able to produce moral *beliefs*, which I doubt . . .
   a. The morality people believed in because of evolution could only be relativistic morality since it is based on beliefs on the inside of people, not based on facts outside in the world. Evolution, then—even in principle—can never produce objective morality.
   b. Therefore, evolution cannot explain the existence of the kind of morality that needs explaining, the kind of morality necessary to make sense of the problem of evil—which everyone, even atheists, agree is a problem.

[?] Self-Assessment

Try to answer the following questions without using your notes.

1. Give a quick solution to the deductive problem of evil.
   ➤ It's possible that a good, powerful God might allow evil if he had good _____ to do so.

2. What is the specific strategy we are using here to deal with the atheist's objection to God based on the problem of evil?
   ➤ We are not going to try to explain why a good, powerful God would _____ evil. Instead, we're going to show that there can't be any _____ of evil in the first place unless God _____.

3. Answering the challenge of the problem of evil trades on two facts that are embedded in the objection itself. What are they?
   ➤ The first fact is that the problem of evil is _____ and _____ knows it. Something is terribly _____ with the world. The second fact is that the evil that people are concerned with is _____ evil, not just that things happen that they don't personally _____ or approve of.

4. Why can't there be a problem of evil if relativism is true?
   > According to relativism, there are no moral _____ governing the world. If that's true, then there are no moral laws to be _____. Therefore, there can't be a problem of evil in the world.

5. How does the existence of objective morality provide evidence for the existence of God?
   > You can't have objective, transcendent laws that are broken, causing the problem of evil, if you do not have a _____ lawmaker.

6. Give the moral argument for God's existence in its simple form.
   > If there is no _____, there is no _____ morality. However, there is objective _____. We know this because of the _____ of evil. Therefore, there is a _____.

7. What is a standard opening question when someone raises the issue of the problem of evil?
   > A good opening question is "What exactly is the _____, as you see it?"

8. What is a good question to use to find out what an atheist means by "evil" when he raises the problem of evil as an objection?
   > The question is "When you raise the issue of evil in the world, do you mean _____ evil—things that are really _____ in themselves—or do you mean _____ evil, things that are only _____ for you?"

9. What is the main thing Christopher Hitchens missed when he challenged believers to show him one good thing they could do as theists that he couldn't do as an atheist?
   > It does not matter if an atheist can do all the same _____ or actions that theists call good. The issue is whether those behaviors can be genuinely _____ good if there is no _____.

10. Explain the writer/reader analogy to make this point.

- People who don't believe in writers can still _____ just fine, but there would be _____ to read if _____ didn't exist. In the same way, an atheist can do the same _____ a theist can, but those behaviors wouldn't be _____ for either atheist or theist if there was no _____ to account for or ground _____ to begin with.

11. What was the second problem with Hitchens's challenge?
    - An atheist simply _____ do all the good things a theist can do. He can never _____ or give glory to God, which is the _____ good according to Christian morality. Simply put, the atheist and the theist do not share the _____ morality.

12. Even if Darwinism were true, why is it inadequate to provide an explanation for morality given the problem of evil?
    - Even if true, Darwinian evolution can only account for beliefs about morality that are _____ a person. It cannot explain moral facts on the _____. Since Darwinism can only produce _____, relativistic morality, it cannot account for the _____ morality that is necessary to make sense of the problem of evil.

13. What is the word that atheistic philosophers use to describe morality that is the result of evolution?
    - Careful philosophers acknowledge that if evolution is responsible for morality then morality is an _____.

14. What, then, is the proper conclusion about the problem of evil if evolution is an accurate explanation of our beliefs about morality?
    - If evolution is an accurate explanation of our beliefs about morality, then the proper conclusion is that there is no _____ of evil.

☑ Self-Assessment with Answers

1. It's possible that a good, powerful God might allow evil if he had good **reason** to do so.

2. We are not going to try to explain why a good, powerful God would **allow** evil. Instead, we're going to show that there can't be any **problem** of evil in the first place unless God **exists**.
3. The first fact is that the problem of evil is **real** and **everyone** knows it. Something is terribly **wrong** with the world. The second fact is that the evil that people are concerned with is **objective** evil, not just that things happen that they don't personally **like** or approve of.
4. According to relativism, there are no moral **laws** governing the world. If that's true, then there are no moral laws to be **broken**. Therefore, there can't be a problem of evil in the world.
5. You can't have objective, transcendent laws that are broken, causing the problem of evil, if you do not have a **transcendent** lawmaker.
6. If there is no **God**, there is no **objective** morality. However, there is objective **morality**. We know this because of the **problem** of evil. Therefore, there is a **God**.
7. A good opening question is "What exactly is the **problem**, as you see it?"
8. The question is "When you raise the issue of evil in the world, do you mean **objective** evil—things that are really **wrong** in themselves—or do you mean **relativistic** evil, things that are only **wrong** for you?"
9. It does not matter if an atheist can do all the same **behaviors** or actions that theists call good. The issue is whether those behaviors can be genuinely **objectively** good if there is no **God**.
10. People who don't believe in writers can still **read** just fine, but there would be **nothing** to read if **writers** didn't exist. In the same way, an atheist can do the same **behaviors** a theist can, but those behaviors wouldn't be **good** for either atheist or theist if there was no **God** to account for or ground **morality** to begin with.
11. An atheist simply **can't** do all the good things a theist can do. He can never **worship** or give glory to God, which is the **greatest** good according to Christian morality. Simply put, the atheist and the theist do not share the **same** morality.

12. Even if true, Darwinian evolution can only account for beliefs about morality that are **inside** a person. It cannot explain moral facts on the **outside**. Since Darwinism can only produce **internal**, relativistic morality, it cannot account for the **objective** morality that is necessary to make sense of the problem of evil.
13. Careful philosophers acknowledge that if evolution is responsible for morality, then morality is an **illusion**.
14. If evolution is an accurate explanation of our beliefs about morality, then the proper conclusion is that there is no **problem** of evil.

Interactive Group Study Questions

1. Talk about why the problem of evil is one of the most formidable challenges to the existence of God for many people.
2. Discuss some reasons why a good and powerful God might allow evil in the world.
3. Why does Greg call the problem of evil "atheism's fatal flaw"? How is the presence of evil in the world actually evidence for God's existence?
4. Discuss the two facts that are embedded in the challenge of evil itself that we can use to make our case for God's existence.
5. Discuss how the problem of evil is incompatible with relativism. How does real evil require morality to be objective rather than subjective?
6. Discuss the careful distinction theists must make when atheists say they can be good without God. How does the relationship of writers to readers illustrate why there can be no objective goodness without God?
7. According to Darwinism, how does evolution work to create morality? Why do you think moral beliefs caused by natural selection fail to explain actual genuine good and evil?

Going Deeper: Information for Self-Study

1. Explain to a friend the things you learned in this lesson.
   - Explain why the existence of evil is actually evidence for God, not against him.

- Then rehearse the specific reasons why evolution is not adequate to explain the kind of morality—objective morality—that needs explaining.
- Also explain why atheists are not able to do the very same "good" things theists can do.

2. If you have a friend who is an atheist who thinks there really is a problem of evil, ask him in a friendly way about how he accounts for the objective morality that makes the problem of evil possible.

3. Be prepared to share your experiences with the group when you get together next time.

 Food for Thought

What People Can't Not Know

The existence of evil is *psychologically* daunting for theists, but it's not the *rational* problem most people think it is. Indeed, for Christians, evil is an ally if they know how to leverage the problem in their favor.

For all their don't-push-your-morality-on-me protests, most people know better. Deep down inside, they are certain that some things are bad *in themselves*. Count on that. This fact about the problem of evil leads to an insight lethal to atheism.

In *The Brothers Karamazov*, Fyodor Dostoyevsky famously noted that if God does not exist, then all is permitted. If there is no lawmaker—God—there can be no law: nothing properly forbidden and nothing required. If no law, then no law *breaking*—thus no evil—and no law *keeping*, either—thus no good. Behaviors just are, and—for the intellectually honest atheist—nothing more can be said about them.

A Candid Admission from Richard Dawkins

According to atheist Richard Dawkins, if there is no God, then there is no transcendent plan, no ultimate purpose, and no morality. Note his blunt admission: "In a universe of electrons and selfish genes, blind physical forces and genetic replication, some people are going to get hurt, other people are going to get lucky, and you won't find any rhyme or reason in it, nor any justice. The universe that we observe has the properties we should expect if there is, at bottom, no design, no purpose, no evil, no good, nothing but blind, pitiless indifference."[9]

The Main Point

You have probably noticed I've been making the same point in a number of different ways. For clarity's sake, then, let me revisit my main point in sum. Here it is in a nutshell.

The problem of evil is only a problem if evil is real—obviously. To say something is evil, though, is to make a moral judgment—also obvious. Moral judgments require a moral standard—a moral law—and a moral law requires an author. If the standard is transcendent, then the lawgiver must be transcendent, too.

If there is a problem of evil (and there is), then God exists. He is the best explanation for the way things are—*even for the problem of evil*. That is why evil is atheism's fatal flaw.

The Theist's Bonus

If the moral law is good—which it must be since its violation is clearly evil—then the one from whom those laws emerge is probably good, as well. Bitter springs do not produce sweet water.

This is the theist's bonus. The problem of evil does not just give us objective morality *grounded* in God. It also gives us *a good* God. There is perfect goodness because someone is perfectly good. A good God made the world a certain way, the way it's supposed to be. Our fallen desires drive us toward a different end. God wants the good for us, and we do not. The problem is with us, not with God.

Whatever a good God commands will not just be good in the abstract; it will also be good *for* us. We cannot see into the future to know the consequences of our actions. God can. We do not know how things were meant to work, at least not completely. God does.

With every command, God directs us toward wholeness, helping us be the way we're supposed to be. We are the clay, and he is the Potter. Only under his hand and under the protection of his precepts can we be formed into something beautiful.

---

9. Richard Dawkins, *River out of Eden* (New York: Basic Books, 1995), 133.

SESSION 6

JESUS THE SON, CHRIST THE SAVIOR

Demonstrating Mastery

Try recalling the answers to the following questions without using your notes. The answers are in the "Self-Assessment with Answers" section of session 5.

1. How does the existence of objective morality provide evidence for the existence of God?
2. What is a standard opening question when someone raises the issue of the problem of evil?
3. Even if Darwinism were true, why is it inadequate to provide an explanation for morality given the problem of evil?
4. What, then, is the proper conclusion about the problem of evil if evolution is an accurate explanation of our beliefs about morality?

I. Review and Looking Ahead

A. In the preceding session, we covered the following:

1. First, I showed you how, if relativism is true, then it's impossible for there to be a problem of evil.

a. Real evil happens when real objective moral laws are broken.

b. If there are no objective moral laws, then there can't be any broken laws.

c. If there aren't any broken moral laws, then there is no problem of evil.

2. Second, I showed you how the problem of evil is actually evidence *for* God, not *against* him.

a. Real moral laws—laws that transcend mere human opinion—have to be broken in the world for there to be a real problem of evil.

b. But you can't have transcendent laws that are broken, causing the problem of evil, if you don't have a transcendent lawmaker. That would be God.

3. Finally, we looked at an alternative explanation offered for the existence of morality: Darwinian evolution.

a. First, we learned that even though atheists can mimic the behavior of theists, if God didn't exist, then no behavior—by atheists or theists—could be objectively good or bad.

(1) Just as writers are necessary for books to exist . . .

(2) God is necessary for real goodness to exist.

b. Second, I pointed out that morality without God simply is not the same as morality with God since honoring God is the greatest good in Christian morality. Atheists can't do that.

c. Third, we learned that even if evolution were able to produce moral *beliefs*, which I doubt . . .

(1) The morality people believed in because of evolution could only be relativistic morality since it is based on beliefs on the inside of people, not based on facts outside in the world. Evolution, then—even in principle—can never produce objective morality.

(2) Therefore, evolution cannot explain the existence of the kind of morality that needs explaining, the kind of morality necessary to make sense of the problem of evil—which everyone, even atheists, agree is a problem.

B. Here is what we'll cover in this session:

1. First, I'll make the case that Jesus was a true man of history.

2. Second, I'll show why scripturally it makes sense that Jesus and the Father are separate persons, but both are fully God, even though there's only one God. The Trinity is not a contradiction.
3. Next, I'll tell why Jesus' claim to be the Son of God was actually a claim to *be* God, even if he didn't actually use the words "I am God."
4. Finally, I'll show why Jesus is the only Savior for the world.

II. The Early Days

A. **When I was a young Christian in the early 1970s, I wore a necklace identifying me as a Christian.**
  1. It was called an *ichthus*, the Greek word for "fish." It consisted of two intersecting arcs forming the silhouette of a fish. Sometimes you see it on bumper stickers or in ads by Christians.
  2. The Greek word inside the body of the fish summarized the ancient Christians' core theology about Jesus of Nazareth. The Greek letters stood for Jesus, Christ, God's Son, Savior. That summed up four vital pieces of the Christian message about Jesus. The man Jesus was the Messiah (the "Christ"), God's only Son, the Savior.
  3. It's a handy summary of the essentials of Christian theology regarding Jesus of Nazareth:
      a. Jesus was a true human being.
      b. He was God's promised "Anointed One," the Christ.
      c. He was no mere mortal, though. He was God's own Son.
          (1) God in human flesh, in other words
          (2) God come down, "Immanuel"—God with us
      d. He was also the chosen Savior of the world.

B. **Every detail of this ancient creed is under siege today.**
  1. Was Jesus a true man of history?

2. Was he merely the Son of God and not God himself?

3. Was he the Christ, the world's one and only Savior?

III. The Problem of Jesus, the Man

A. The first issue we face is whether Jesus even existed.

1. The internet is full of claims that the story of Jesus is a myth. According to that view . . .

    a. The Gospels are sophisticated plagiarisms.

    b. They consist of details pilfered from ancient myths about deities like Osiris, Adonis, Mithras, Horus, and others.

    c. They were then cobbled together to fabricate the story of the dying and rising god/man from Nazareth.

2. I don't have space here to list all the problems with this claim,[1] but here's a quick summary:

    a. When you consult the primary source documents for those legends, you'll discover . . .

        (1) The online details of those ancient myths are not entirely accurate (it's the internet, after all).

        (2) There are almost no genuine parallels between those gods of legend and Jesus.

        (3) The records of some of the ancient myths do not *predate* the time of Christ. They come afterward, and the life of Christ, then, could not have been copied from them.

        (4) Even when those records do predate the time of Christ, the details in those myths do not prove that the Gospels are fiction. That must be determined on independent historical grounds.

    b. Is Jesus just a mythical, copycat messiah? The conclusion from the actual evidence is: not a chance.[2]

---

1. I covered this issue thoroughly in *The Story of Reality* (Grand Rapids: Zondervan, 2017), ch. 16.

2. For an in-depth analysis, see Ronald Nash, *The Gospel and the Greeks: Did the New Testament Borrow from Pagan*

B. **One reason we can be completely confident is that we have records from secular historians of that time verifying the basic historical details of Jesus' life.**
   1. At least seventeen ancient secular sources, along with lots of archaeological evidence, confirm the accuracy of the Gospels as a testimony of Jesus as a man of history.[3]
   2. People like Josephus, Tacitus, Pliny the Younger, and Lucian, among others
   3. From just four of those sources we learn: there was a virtuous man named Jesus . . . who had a brother named James. . . . Jesus was crucified under Pontius Pilate . . . during the reign of Tiberius Caesar . . . and was reported to be alive three days later . . . and the multitude who followed him were called Christians and worshiped him as a god.

C. **"Jesus never existed"?**
   1. There simply is no lettered person in the field who believes that. I got that detail from one of Christianity's most vocal *critics*: historian Bart Ehrman.[4]
   2. The story that Jesus is a myth is itself the real myth.

Reflect a Moment

That the Jesus of the Gospels is a hodgepodge compilation of ancient deities and not a notable figure in history is a complete fiction thoroughly discredited by experts in the field. The only place this notion survives is on the internet, not in the academy proper.

So that's the first challenge. Here's the second:

IV. The Problem of Jesus, the God

A. **How could Jesus be God when there's only one God, and God is in heaven and Jesus is on earth?**

Thought? 2nd ed. (Phillipsburg, NJ: P&R, 2003); or Lee Strobel, *The Case for the Real Jesus: A Journalist Investigates Current Attacks on the Identity of Christ* (Grand Rapids: Zondervan, 2007).

3. Gary Habermas, *The Verdict of History* (Nashville: Thomas Nelson, 1988), 108.

4. Bart Ehrman, "The Historical Jesus Did Exist," YouTube, accessed May 31, 2023, https://www.youtube.com/watch?v=43mDuIN5-ww.

This, of course, is the challenge of the Trinity (leaving the Holy Spirit out of this discussion for the sake of simplicity). Since all the information we have on this issue is from Scripture, we have to go to Scripture for an answer.

B. Here is the problem we find in Scripture:
1. First, there is only one God.
2. Second, Jesus is a distinct person from the Father.
    a. Jesus interacts with the Father in personal ways.
    b. He prays to the Father, he submits to the Father, the Father speaks when Jesus is present listening, and so on.
3. Finally, Jesus is fully God. We know this because . . .
    a. He is called God a number of times in the text.
    b. He has divine attributes (for example, he was the uncreated Creator, John 1:3).
    c. He exercises divine privileges (for example, he received worship).
4. These awkward facts are what led the early church to conclude:
    a. Although God is one in essence (strict monotheism) . . .
    b. He is more than one in person—he has more than one center of consciousness.
    c. He is one "what" and three "whos," so to speak.
    d. That is the only way to resolve what at first seems to be an unsolvable contradiction.
5. Thus, the Trinity turns out to be a solution, not a problem, because it's the only way to understand Scripture that harmonizes all the parts.

> **Ambassador Skills**
>
> Here is a similar complaint you'll encounter: according to Christians, since Jesus is God, when he prayed to God he was only praying to himself. Note, though, that when you and I pray to God, we don't pray to his *nature*. We speak to God's person: "our *Father*." In that same sense, the person of Jesus, the Son, could pray to the person of God the Father without contradiction or confusion. He was not praying to himself.

6. Here's what a dialogue with a unitarian might look like (a unitarian is a person who believes there is one God who is only one person, like a Jehovah's Witness):

> "I know you object to the Trinity, but could you please tell me exactly why?"

"Because the Bible teaches there's only one God."

> "I agree."

"No, you don't. You believe in the Trinity."

> "Right. But believing in one God is part of the definition of the Trinity."

"But you think the Father, Son, and Spirit are all God. That's three gods, not one."

> "Actually, our view is a little different from that. Our view is that the one God has three separate centers of consciousness—one 'what' and three 'whos,' so to speak."

"But that doesn't make sense. Who did Jesus pray to if he's God? Nobody prays to himself."

> "You're right. Jesus didn't pray to himself. He prayed to the Father."

"So you admit that Jesus is different from the Father."

> "Of course I do. That's part of the definition of the Trinity."

"Don't you see how confused that is?"

> "Confused? Didn't you just tell me you agreed with me so far?"

"How?"

> "Well, you said you believe the Bible teaches there is only one God, right?"

"Yes."

> "So do I. You also agree that Jesus is different from the Father, right?"

"Right."

> "Then, so far we are in complete agreement on what the Bible teaches. Are you with me?"

"Sure. But you also believe Jesus is God."

> "Right, but what if I could show you the Bible actually teaches that?"

"But it doesn't."

"Can I give you one example? Who is the creator of everything that's ever been created?"

"Jehovah. Isaiah 44:24: 'I, the LORD, am the maker of all things . . . by Myself . . . all alone.'"

"Right. I agree. Good verse: 'I, *the* LORD . . . by *Myself* . . . all *alone*.' By the way, when John talks about the Word in the beginning of John 1, who is he talking about?"

"He means the one who was born as Jesus: 'The Word became flesh, and dwelt among us,' John 1:14."

"Exactly. But John 1:3 also says that the Word created all things that were ever created: 'All things came into being through Him, and apart from Him nothing came into being that has come into being.' Have you read that before?"

"Sounds familiar."

"So, if the Bible teaches that Jehovah was the only Creator, and it also teaches that a different person, the Word, was the Creator, then you have a contradiction. So how do you solve that problem?"

"I'm not sure."

"This is why the early church used the word *Trinity*: three distinct persons all sharing the same single divine nature. It solves the problem."

> **Ambassador Skills**
>
> Note that in conversations like these, I'm alert for anything the other person says that I can genuinely agree with. Doing so is fair-minded and evenhanded, and it also keeps the conversation amicable.

7. Notice, by the way, that I'm not trying to prove that Jesus actually is divine.
    a. That requires other evidence—like the resurrection, for example.
    b. I'm merely trying to show that the authoritative Christian record—the New Testament—teaches that Jesus is uniquely divine.

V. Cosmic Confusion

A. Sometimes the complaint about the Trinity comes from people who have no interest in Scripture.
   1. To them, the Trinity just doesn't make sense.
   2. The three-in-one formula seems to them to be a contradiction.

B. Not all three-in-ones are contradictions, though.
   1. There are three angles in one triangle, yet no one balks at this concept.
   2. One family can have three members: Dad, Mom, and little Johnny. No problem there, either.
   3. These are not illustrations of the Trinity. They're just a way of showing that three-in-ones are not necessarily contradictions.

Here's why:

C. As long as the precise way a thing is three is different from the way it is one, there's no problem.
   1. Jesus is distinct from the Father in one way (in his person), but the same in another way (in his divine essence). Weird? Yes. Contradictory? No. That doesn't prove that the Trinity is true, but it does show it's not false in virtue of contradiction.
   2. Here is how a conversation about that might look:

   > "The Trinity doesn't make sense."
   >> "Really? Why not?" [Columbo #1]
   >
   > "It's a contradiction."
   >> "Can you tell me specifically what the contradiction is?" [Note more Columbo #1 requests for clarification.]
   >
   > "Because you can't have three in one. It's a contradiction. You have three gods and one God at the same time. That's nonsense."
   >> "You're right. That would be nonsense if that's what we meant by the Trinity. Let me ask you a question. How many people are in your family?"

"Four. My wife, me, and our two kids. Why?"

"So, you have four people in your family? You have four in one? Impossible. That's a contradiction. If you can't have three in one, how can you have four in one?"

"That's different."

"How?"

"Because a family is one thing, and the people who make up that family are another thing. They're not the same, so there's no contradiction."

"Exactly. That's my point. As long as the one (one family) is different from the four (four people), you're in the clear, right?"

"That's right."

"The same with the Trinity. When Christians talk about the Trinity, they mean the one (one God) is different from the three (three persons). Do you see how that's not a contradiction?"

"Well, you've got a point, but that doesn't make it true."

"You're right. It doesn't. But it does show it's not contradictory, right?"

VI. "I am God. Worship Me."

A. Some people, especially Muslims, raise the point that Jesus never actually said, "I am God." Others say that Jesus never claimed to be God, only the Son of God.

1. As far as we know, Jesus never uttered those exact words. But why does that matter?
2. If I said, "Here are my daughters, Annabeth and Eva," but never said, "I am a parent," would it be fair to say I never claimed to be a parent? Of course not. There's more than one way of indicating I'm a parent.

B. In Jesus' case, he said lots of things that made his divine claim clear to the first-century Jews he was speaking to.

1. By calling God his Father and saying he was the Son of God, Jesus was asserting equality with God. The Jews understood that perfectly. They said, "You, being a man, *make Yourself out to be God*" (John 10:33, emphasis added).[5]

---

5. See also John 5:18; 8:56–59; 19:7; and Mark 2:5–7.

2. This blasphemy was a capital crime[6] (the same as it would be in Islam, by the way) and was the precise reason the Jewish court had Jesus executed:

> The high priest was questioning Him. . . , "Are You the Christ, the Son of the Blessed One?"
>
> And Jesus said, "I am." . . .
>
> The high priest said, "You have heard the blasphemy." And they all condemned Him to be deserving of death. (Mark 14:61–64)

3. Jesus was not condemned for claiming to be the Messiah. Jesus blasphemed by claiming he was the Son of the Blessed One—God himself.
4. Again, this doesn't prove Jesus was God, but it's clear he made the claim—in multiple ways on multiple occasions.
5. To unpack that point, here's how a conversation might look—in this case, talking with a Muslim:

> "Where did Jesus ever say, 'I am God'? He never did."
>
> "Well, I think you're right about Jesus not using those exact words. But let me ask you a question. Is that the only way someone could claim to be God? Could Jesus claim to be God using other words?"
>
> "How could he do that?"
>
> "As a Muslim yourself, what would you think it meant if someone used the sacred Jewish name for God and applied it to himself?"
>
> "Did Jesus do that?"
>
> "Yes. He said, 'Before Abraham was born, I am.' That's God's name for himself right out of the burning bush in Exodus. What if one of his closest followers claimed he created everything that was ever created?"
>
> "Where is that?"

---

6. Leviticus 24:16.

"That's in John 1:3. What if Jesus never said, 'Worship me,' but he still received worship from others?"

"That would be pretty bad."

"Well, you can find that in Matthew 14. There are half a dozen verses like this in the Gospels.[7] One last thing."

"What's that?"

"Do you know why Jesus was executed?"

"Well, he made the Jews mad."

"He sure did. You can read in the historical account of his trial about *why* they were mad. Jesus was sentenced to death for blasphemy, for claiming to be the Son of God—which the Jews clearly understood as a claim to be God."

"I didn't know that."

"So, one, he was identified as the Creator of everything that ever was created; two, he applied the unique, holy name of God to himself; three, he received worship from men; and four, he was executed for blasphemy for claiming to be the Son of God. Is it fair to say that's pretty close to saying, 'I am God'?"

6. Here's a way you might clarify the "Jesus only claimed to be the Son of God" confusion:

"What if I said a person was gay. What would you think I meant?"

"That he was a homosexual, of course."

"But what if I then said, 'He's not a homosexual; he's *gay*. He's the most cheerful guy I know.' What would you say?"

"I'd say that's confused."

"I agree. It's confused to our ears in the twenty-first century. A hundred years ago, though, those words would have made perfect sense, because back then the word *gay* meant something completely different."

---

7. For a complete treatment of this point, see "Was Jesus Worshiped?" Stand to Reason, June 26, 2019, https://www.str.org/search?q=was+jesus+worshiped%3F.

"So, what's your point?"

"The point is, when we read the words of ancient people, we need to understand those words according to *their* meaning then, not *our* meaning now."

"Okay."

"So how do you think that relates to your claim that Jesus was not God, but the Son of God?"

"I don't follow you."

"I'm asking what Jesus' claim to be the Son of God meant to the people who heard him in his day."

"How would we know?"

"Here's how: they tried to kill him because they said he was claiming to be God."

7. So, according to the New Testament, Jesus is the Son of God in a way no other "child of God" can be—the Son of God is God the Son.

Reflect a Moment

That God humbled himself, stepped down, and took on human flesh is a detail so familiar to Christendom that the luster is often lost. Yet it is no minor matter. It is not a dispensable footnote in the biblical record, a negligible twist of Christian theology. Rather, it is central to the grand story of reality the biblical text tells, and it is central to the claim that Jesus alone saves.

Now I'd like to show you why this man, God's Son, is also God's Christ—the world's only possible Savior.

VII. Christ the Savior

A. The word *Christ* is the Anglicized version of the Greek word *Christos*.
  1. It means "Anointed One" or "Messiah."
  2. Messiah is a uniquely Jewish concept.
  3. Even so, God intended for this Messiah—this rescuer—to provide rescue not just for Jews but also for the whole world (Gen. 12:3).

B. **The stumbling stone**
   1. Probably the most offensive detail of our Christian message is that a person must put his trust in Jesus—and only Jesus—to escape eternal punishment for his sin. Peter called it "a stone of stumbling and a rock of offense" (1 Peter 2:8, quoting Isa. 8:14). It is also gospel bedrock.
   2. To stand with Jesus on this issue invites a tsunami of scorn and abuse from others.
      a. The pressure to treat all religions as equally valid routes to God is a tremendous incentive to modify the Christian message. Do not do it. To side with the crowd on this is spiritual treason.
      b. Sometimes singular problems (the problem of sin and evil) require singular solutions. No other message can cure man's malady.

C. **I found a hundred verses in the New Testament that teach—explicitly or implicitly—that faith in Christ is the only hope of salvation.**[8] **Here are three of them:**
   1. Jesus said, "I am the way, and the truth, and the life; no one comes to the Father but through Me" (John 14:6).
   2. Peter said, "There is salvation in no one else; for there is no other name under heaven that has been given among men by which we must be saved" (Acts 4:12).
   3. Paul, when asked by the Philippian jailer, "What must I do to be saved?" gave only one answer, "Believe in the Lord Jesus, and you will be saved" (Acts 16:30–31).

D. **But *why* is Jesus the only way of salvation?**
   1. Jesus is the only way of salvation because he is the only one who solved the problem. Indeed, he is the only one who could.
   2. We cannot rescue ourselves. Rescue must come from outside our world.

E. **Precisely how does Messiah rescue the world?**
   1. Here's how: he paid so we wouldn't have to.
   2. At the final judgment, every person who ever lived will receive one of two things, either perfect justice—punishment for everything they've ever done wrong—or perfect mercy—forgiveness for everything they've ever done wrong.

---
8. See *Jesus, the Only Way: 100 Verses* (Signal Hill, CA: Stand to Reason, 2009).

a. If *Jesus* didn't pay for their crimes (perfect mercy), then *they* will have to pay for their crimes (perfect justice).
b. That's the sobering calculus.

F. **Remember, the idea that Jesus is the only way of salvation is *his* claim about himself; it's not *our* claim about him.**
1. We didn't make this up. We are merely repeating what Jesus said many times over in many ways.
2. So, when people push back on your "arrogant" claim, put it on Jesus. Try something like this:

"You Christians think your way is the only right way."
"We do, but why is that a problem?" [Columbo #1]
"It's so arrogant!"
"Can I ask you a question?"
"Sure."
"Where do you think that idea came from?"
"It came from arrogant, narrow-minded Christians."
"Well, actually, it came from Jesus himself. Do you think Jesus was arrogant and narrow-minded?"
"Of course not. He was a great man who taught love and acceptance."
"He also taught he was the only way to heaven, and he said it many times in many ways. So, I'm just curious, do you think Jesus was mistaken?"

Ambassador Skills

Character attack—simple name-calling—is the go-to response for virtually every controversial opinion raised in this culture, unfortunately. It happens so frequently that those who do it don't realize they're out of order—both in reasoning and in manners.

3. Here's another:

   "You're arrogant to think your way is the only right way."

   "I don't mean to be rude, but that strikes me as an odd response."

   "Why?"

   "Let me try to explain why with an illustration."

   "Okay."

   "Let's say you go with a friend to a doctor and the doctor says your friend needs a precise treatment or he'll die. Your friend then says to the doctor, 'You're mean. I'm going to find another doctor who's not so mean.' What would you think of your friend if he did that?"

   "I'd think it was pretty dumb."

   "Why?"

   "Well, even if the doctor was mean—and he probably wasn't—his diagnosis still could be correct."

   "Good point. What else?"

   "It's also dumb because my friend might really be sick, and if he doesn't get help, he'll die."

   "Exactly. I agree. Now let me change the illustration just a bit. A Christian tells you that you're dying of a spiritual disease called sin and only Jesus can cure it, and you say he's mean—or more specifically, he's arrogant. How is that any different from the guy in the illustration?"

4. This analogy is a good one because . . .
   a. When a nonbeliever points out an apparent character flaw in the Christian ("You're arrogant") . . .
   b. It keeps him from considering the possibility that the Christian's diagnosis is correct.

5. Here's a final dialogue on this issue:

   "You Christians think you're the only ones who have the truth. That's arrogant."

"I don't understand. Why am I arrogant just because I've thought about an issue and come to a conclusion I think is correct?"

"Because you think everyone else is wrong but you. That's pretty egotistical."

"Do you mind if I ask you a question about that?"

"Go ahead."

"What do *you* think is the right way to get to heaven, or to please God, or however you want to put it? Do you have an opinion?"

"Well, I think being a good, kind, loving person is the answer. I think that's what religion is all about."

"Well, I agree that God cares about that, but you sound like you're convinced that being good is the one thing that matters. Did I get you right, or am I missing something?"

"Yep. Being a good person is what counts."

"That's confusing."

"Why?"

"Because you were just faulting me because I thought *my* way was right, but it turns out *you* think your own way is right. Aren't you doing the same thing you were telling me not to do? I'm not bothered by it, but it does make me wonder. Why is it okay for you to think you're right on religion, but it's not okay for me to think I'm right on religion?"

VIII. What Main Points Did We Cover in This Session?

A. First, I made the case that Jesus was a true man of history.
1. There is virtually no similarity between the myths of ancient gods—like Osiris, Adonis, Mithras, and Horus—and the details of the life of Jesus of Nazareth.
2. A wealth of secular historical material from the time clearly confirms important facts about Jesus that we find in the Gospels.

B. Second, I showed why scripturally it makes sense that Jesus and the Father are separate persons, but both are fully God, even though there's only one God.

1. The Father and the Son interact with each other in personal ways.
2. They are both called God and have attributes unique to God.
3. But there's still only one God.

C. **I then showed why that is not a contradiction.**
   1. It's not a contradiction because the Father and the Son are distinct in a different way from the way they are the same.
   2. Jesus is distinct from the Father in his person.
   3. But he is the same as the Father in his divine essence.

D. **Next, I showed why Jesus' claim to be the Son of God was actually a claim to *be* God, even if he didn't actually use the words "I am God."**
   1. In the language of the Jews, claiming to be the Son of God was claiming to be God the Son.
   2. That's exactly why Jesus was executed: he claimed deity for himself.

E. **Fifth, I showed how Scripture clearly teaches that Jesus is the only way of salvation.**
   1. Jesus taught this truth.
   2. So did all those Jesus personally trained to take his message after him.

F. **Finally, I told you *why* Jesus is the only way of salvation: he's the only one who solved the problem.**
   1. When people stand before God in judgment, either Jesus pays for their sins, or they will pay.
   2. Either perfect mercy or perfect justice.

ⓘ Self-Assessment

Try to answer the following questions without using your notes.

1. What are the four vital pieces of information about Jesus that are represented in the Greek acronym contained in the ichthus?

➤ First, Jesus was a _____ man of history. Second, Jesus was the "_____" One, the _____. Third, Jesus was _____ the _____. Fourth, Jesus was the only _____ of the world.

2. One challenge to Christianity is the claim that the story of Jesus was a sophisticated plagiarism copied from ancient pagan legends. List four points against this view.
    ➤ One, the online details of those ancient myths are not entirely _____. Two, there are almost no genuine _____ between those gods of legend and Jesus. Three, the records of some of the ancient myths do not _____ the time of Christ. Four, even when those records do predate the time of Christ, the _____ in those myths do not prove that the Gospels are fictions.

3. Why can we have confidence that Jesus was a true man of history even if we don't have the Gospels?
    ➤ We can construct most of the critical details of Jesus' life from ancient _____ sources.

4. Why is the Trinity a scriptural solution, not a problem?
    ➤ The Trinity is a solution, not a problem, because it's the only way to understand the _____ in Scripture about God and Jesus that _____ all the parts.

5. Give three reasons how we know from Scripture that Jesus is God.
    ➤ One, Jesus is _____ God. Two, Jesus has divine _____. Three, Jesus exercises divine _____.

6. What is a simple way to describe the Trinity?
    ➤ God is one "_____" and three "_____."

7. Why is the Trinity—God as three in one—not a contradiction when accurately understood?
    ➤ The Trinity is not a contradiction because God is _____ in a different way than he is _____. God is one in essence or _____ and three in _____.

8. Why is the observation that Jesus never said "I am God; worship me" not a good reason to think Jesus didn't claim divinity for himself?
   ▸ Because there are more ways of claiming to be _____ than simply saying, "I am God."

9. What are four ways Jesus did claim divinity for himself?
   ▸ One, he called God his _____, claiming _____ with God. Two, Jesus was executed for claiming to be the _____ of God, which was _____. Three, Jesus used the sacred _____ of God and applied it to _____. Four, Jesus readily received _____ from others.

10. In a sentence and simply put, why is Jesus the only way of salvation?
    ▸ Jesus is the only way of salvation because he is the _____ one who solved the _____.

11. Precisely how does Messiah rescue the world?
    ▸ He _____ for our _____ against God so we wouldn't have to. Either Jesus _____ (perfect mercy) or we _____ (perfect justice).

12. What is a good way to parry being criticized for claiming Jesus is the only way?
    ▸ Put the claim back on _____, since _____ was the one who said he was the _____ way.

☑ **Self-Assessment with Answers**

1. First, Jesus was a **true** man of history. Second, Jesus was the **"Anointed"** One, the **Christ**. Third, Jesus was **God** the **Son**. Fourth, Jesus was the only **Savior** of the world.
2. One, the online details of those ancient myths are not entirely **accurate**. Two, there are almost no genuine **parallels** between those gods of legend and Jesus. Three, the records of some of the ancient myths do not **predate** the time of Christ. Four, even when those records do predate the time of Christ, the **details** in those myths do not prove that the Gospels are fictions.

3. We can construct most of the critical details of Jesus' life from ancient **historical** sources.
4. The Trinity is a solution, not a problem, because it's the only way to understand the **statements** in Scripture about God and Jesus that **harmonize** all the parts.
5. One, Jesus is **called** God. Two, Jesus has divine **attributes**. Three, Jesus exercises divine **privileges**.
6. God is one "**what**" and three "**whos**."
7. The Trinity is not a contradiction because God is **one** in a different way than he is **three**. God is one in essence or **nature** and three in **persons**.
8. Because there are more ways of claiming to be **divine** than simply saying, "I am God."
9. One, he called God his **Father**, claiming **equality** with God. Two, Jesus was executed for claiming to be the **Son** of God, which was **blasphemy**. Three, Jesus used the sacred **name** of God and applied it to **himself**. Four, Jesus readily received **worship** from others.
10. Jesus is the only way of salvation because he is the **only** one who solved the **problem**.
11. He **paid** for our **crimes** against God so we wouldn't have to. Either Jesus **pays** (perfect mercy) or we **pay** (perfect justice).
12. Put the claim back on **Jesus**, since **Jesus** was the one who said he was the **only** way.

Interactive Group Study Questions

1. Why is the story that Jesus is a myth the real myth? Discuss some of the reasons we can be confident that Jesus was a true man of history.
2. Discuss how Jesus and the Father can both be God when there's only one God. How do we know from Scripture that Jesus is fully God?
3. Address the objection that the doctrine of the Trinity entails three gods, not one God. Describe how the doctrine of the Trinity is a solution, not a problem.
4. Discuss some of the ways Jews in the first century clearly understood Jesus' claim of divinity.
5. Why is Jesus the only way of salvation? Discuss with details why Jesus is the only cure for man's malady?

6. Explain Greg's illustration of the sick friend who thinks his doctor is mean. How does this story help us counter the charge that Christians are narrow-minded and arrogant when they claim Jesus is the only answer?

💡 Going Deeper: Information for Self-Study

Explain to a friend the things you've covered in this lesson.

1. Explain the reasons why we can be confident that Jesus was a true man of history and not a plagiarized myth.
2. Explain why—scripturally—the Trinity is a solution, not a problem, and why it's not contradictory.
3. See if you can explain why the claim "Jesus never said, 'I am God,'" is irrelevant.
4. Finally, see if you can explain in clear terms why Jesus is the only way of salvation.
5. Be prepared to share your experiences with the group when you get together next time.

🍎 Food for Thought

Caesar and Christ

Pulitzer Prize–winning historian Will Durant wrote the most successful work *on* history *in* history, the eleven-volume *The Story of Civilization*. The historical evidence he discovered during his research on Jesus of Nazareth was so compelling, it prompted this conclusion in his volume *Caesar and Christ*: "No one reading these scenes can doubt the reality of the figure behind them. . . . After two centuries of Higher Criticism, the outlines of the life, character, and teaching of Christ remain reasonably clear and constitute the most fascinating feature in the history of Western man."[9]

Cold-Case Christ

Arguing from effect back to probable cause, storied cold-case detective and bestselling author J. Warner Wallace chronicles the explosive impact Jesus of Nazareth had on virtually

---

9. Will Durant, *Caesar and Christ*, vol. 3 of *The Story of Civilization* (New York: Simon & Schuster, 1972), 557.

every quarter of culture—music, art, literature, science, world religion, and so on. Fictional figures simply do not leave such a trail of evidence.[10]

The Uncreated Creator

John 1:3 says, "All things came into being through Him, and apart from Him nothing came into being that has come into being." The "Him," of course, is the Word who became flesh in Jesus of Nazareth (v. 14).

In this verse, John says the same thing in two different ways for emphasis and for clarity. Everything that ever came into being owes its existence to the Word, who caused it all to exist. If the Word caused all created things to *come* into existence, then he must have existed *before* all created things *came* into existence. Therefore, the Word could not have been created.

By contrast, if the Word created everything that has come into being, and he also came into being (as some contend), then the Word created himself. But this is impossible. He would have to exist as Creator before he could exist as a created thing, which is absurd. Therefore, the one called the Word who took on humanity in Jesus was the uncreated Creator of all things. Jesus is God.

Myths Don't Make It

The humanity of Jesus as a historical fact is central to the Christian story. Take all other religious leaders and remove them from history, and their religions remain since it is the teachings—not the founders—that ground their faith. If those founders are fictions, the teachings remain with full force.

Not so with Jesus. Take Jesus out of Christianity, and Christianity disappears. Some suggest that nothing is lost if Jesus never existed since the marvelous story remains. Paul disagreed. If Jesus' resurrection is a myth, he said, and the witnesses traded in lies, then Christians are a pitiful lot.[11] And they're fools, too, I might add, since it cost many of them their lives.

Everything essential to our convictions about Christ relies on Jesus being a genuine man of history. It is not surprising, then, that so much ink has been spilled to deny it.

---

10. See J. Warner Wallace, *Person of Interest* (Grand Rapids: Zondervan, 2021).
11. 1 Corinthians 15:17–19.

These efforts fail, though, as I've shown. Nothing in the record suggests that Christians have misplaced their confidence.

Cosmic Child Abuse?

The most famous verse in the Bible is John 3:16: "For God so loved the world, that He gave His only begotten Son, that whoever believes in Him shall not perish, but have eternal life." This noble truth, though, raises a concern.

Do Christians claim that God took a man who was *not* guilty and treated him as if he *were* guilty, that he made him suffer a brutal death as an expression of God's love in pardoning those who *actually were* the guilty ones?

How could savaging the innocent on behalf of the guilty be an act of divine benevolence ("For *God* so loved the world")? How does this kind of God escape the charge of "cosmic child abuse"?

Here's how. Humans were guilty, so a human had to pay. Yet what kind of human could make a boundless payment adequate to cover the endless punishment due for the sins of the entire world? How does a mere man, Jesus, in the short span of three hours on a cross, pay for an eternity of even *one person's* sin, much less the sins of *anyone* and *everyone* who believes? How is that mathematically possible?

Only Jesus *as God* could turn his sacrifice on a cross into a testament of God's love for the world, since it was God's own blood freely shed by Christ[12] that purchased Christ's church (Acts 20:28).

---

12. John 10:18: "No one has taken it [My life] away from Me, but I lay it down on My own."

SESSION 7

THE BIBLE: ANCIENT WORDS, EVER TRUE?

Demonstrating Mastery

Try recalling the answers to the following questions without using your notes. The answers are in the "Self-Assessment with Answers" section of session 6.

1. What are the four vital pieces of information about Jesus represented in the Greek acronym contained in the ichthus?
2. Why can we have confidence that Jesus was a true man of history even if we don't have the Gospels?
3. Why is the Trinity—God as three in one—not a contradiction when accurately understood?
4. In a sentence and simply put, why is Jesus the only way of salvation? What is a good way to parry being criticized for claiming Jesus is the only way?

I. Review and Looking Ahead

A. In the preceding session, we covered the following:
   1. First, I made the case that Jesus was a true man of history.

a. There is virtually no similarity between the myths of ancient gods—like Osiris, Adonis, Mithras, and Horus—and the details of the life of Jesus of Nazareth.

b. A wealth of secular historical material from the time clearly confirms important facts about Jesus that we find in the Gospels.

2. Second, I showed why scripturally it makes sense that Jesus and the Father are separate persons, but both are fully God, even though there's only one God.

   a. The Father and the Son interact with each other in personal ways.

   b. They are both called God and have attributes unique to God. But there's still only one God.

3. I then showed why that is not a contradiction.

   a. It's not a contradiction because the Father and the Son are distinct in a different way from the way they are the same.

   b. Jesus is distinct from the Father in his person.

   c. But he is the same as the Father in his divine essence.

4. Next, I showed why Jesus' claim to be the Son of God was actually a claim to *be* God, even if he didn't actually use the words "I am God."

   a. In the language of the Jews, claiming to be the Son of God was claiming to be God the Son.

   b. That's exactly why Jesus was executed: he claimed deity for himself.

5. Fifth, I showed how Scripture clearly teaches that Jesus is the only way of salvation.

   a. Jesus taught this truth.

   b. So did all those Jesus personally trained to take his message after him.

6. Finally, I told you *why* Jesus is the only way of salvation: he's the only one who solved the problem.

   a. When people stand before God in judgment, either Jesus pays for their sins, or they will pay.

   b. Either perfect mercy or perfect justice.

B. Here is what we'll cover in this session:

1. First, I'll offer some insight on how to address the issues of inerrancy and alleged Bible contradictions when evangelizing.

2. Second, I'll give you the single most important tip for reading your Bible accurately.

3. Next, I'll talk about the conquest of Canaan and the allegation of genocide and ethnic cleansing in the Old Testament.
4. Finally, I'll clarify some confusion about slavery in the Bible.

II. Two Tips about the Bible

A. First tip: don't argue about inerrancy with non-Christians.
1. I am firmly committed to biblical inerrancy. Scripture is God's Word. It is without error in everything it clearly affirms.
2. However, on *strategic* grounds, I do not argue with nonbelievers on this issue.[1]
   a. First, our claim that the Bible is inerrant often triggers an avalanche of allegations about apparent contradictions and discrepancies.
      (1) Those charges can be answered—and whole tomes have been written doing so—but for most witnessing situations it's an unnecessary distraction.
      (2) If you sidestep the God's-inerrant-Word issue, you'll probably sidestep those challenges, too.
   b. Second, we don't need to convince a skeptic of inerrancy to communicate the gospel effectively and make our case for Christianity.
      (1) The early Christians had no intact New Testament to point to as the inerrant Word of God when they evangelized, yet multitudes responded to their witness.
      (2) The gospel stands or falls not on something written in Scripture, strictly speaking, but on something that happened in history: the death and resurrection of Jesus of Nazareth.
3. Instead of building my case for Christ on inerrancy, I argue that the Gospels are historically reliable.
   a. Christianity stands or falls on facts of history about Jesus.
   b. If the critical events recorded in the Gospels actually took place, then Christianity is on solid ground.

---

1. Inerrancy *is*, however, a critical *in-house* concern, to be sure. When churches abandon a high view of Scripture, central doctrines begin to topple, and Christianity falls into ruin.

🔊 Reflect a Moment

Under God's guidance, the Bible accurately records the historical events that make all the difference, but it's the *events* that secure the truth of Christianity, not the *record* of those events.[2]

4. Here's how I might make those points tactically in a conversation:

    "The Bible is full of contradictions."

    "If that were true—which I'm not conceding here—why would that be significant?"

    "Well, that proves it's not the Word of God."

    "But that's not what I'm arguing here."

    "Don't you think the Bible is God's Word?"

    "Sure I do, but that's not the point I'm making."

    "What's that?"

    "Let me ask you a question. Do you have any books in your library that you think tell you things that are accurate about the world?"

    "Sure."

    "Are any of them divinely inspired?"

    "Of course not."

    "Then a book doesn't need to be divinely inspired to give you truth, does it?"

    "I guess not."

    "So, all I'm asking is that you consider the historical record of Jesus' claims—and the things written by those he trained—to see if they strike you as reasonable or not."

5. So that's the first tip:
    a. Don't waste time arguing with a nonbeliever that the Bible is God's inerrant Word.

---

2. See Paul's statement in 1 Corinthians 15:12–19.

b. Talk with *Christians* about that, for sure, but sidestep that issue with non-Christians.

B. Second tip: never read a Bible verse.

1. If you want to know what an individual verse means, you can't simply read that one verse. You have to read the larger context to capture the flow of thought that gives clarity to the writer's meaning.[3]

    a. This practice is critical for you as a student of the Bible.

    b. It's also critical in dealing with objections about the Bible.

2. To understand the meaning of any text, we need to be clear on . . .

    a. The flow of thought of the passage (its context)

    b. The audience it was written for (its historical/cultural setting and purpose)

    c. The normal conventions of language of that audience (figures of speech, idioms, genre,[4] and so on)[5]

C. Here's why this skill is critical for you as an ambassador for Christ.

1. You'll have friends challenge you on passages of Scripture that they completely misunderstand because . . .

    a. They've missed the context.

    b. Or they were not aware of the cultural setting.

    c. Or they did not observe normal conventions of language of that time.

2. Therefore, they've misunderstood the point the author was making and have created or imagined problems that were not there.[6]

These concerns are especially relevant to the next two challenges.[7]

---

3. There may be times when you'll *quote* an individual verse, of course. I do it all the time. There's nothing wrong with that if you've taken careful stock of the context so you're reasonably confident you're not misrepresenting the author's meaning.

4. Genre refers to the specific kind or category of the writing—history, poetry, parable, and so on.

5. These three are necessary to accurately read writings of any sort. We easily distort the meaning of Scripture if we read it using any other method. Most of the time we should read the Bible the ordinary way.

6. For an accessible, popular book on biblical interpretation, see Gordon Fee and Douglas Stuart, *How to Read the Bible for All Its Worth* (Grand Rapids: Zondervan, 1982). For a superb thorough treatment, see William Klein, Craig Blomberg, and Robert Hubbard Jr., *Introduction to Biblical Interpretation* (Nashville: Thomas Nelson, 1993).

7. Critics raise other issues that, for the sake of space, I cannot cover here. For an excellent, accessible treatment of other problem passages, see Dan Kimball, *How (Not) to Read the Bible: Making Sense of the Anti-women, Anti-science, Pro-violence, Pro-slavery and Other Crazy-Sounding Parts of Scripture* (Grand Rapids: Zondervan, 2020).

III. When God Gets Rough

A. According to critics, the God of the Hebrews was patently immoral. "Just read the Bible," they say. For example:

> When the LORD your God brings you into the land where you are entering to possess it, and clears away many nations before you . . . *you shall utterly destroy them.* (Deut. 7:1–2, emphasis added)

> In the cities of these peoples that the LORD your God is giving you as an inheritance, *you shall not leave alive anything that breathes. But you shall utterly destroy them.* (Deut. 20:16–17, emphasis added)

1. Strong words, and there are more passages like these. They sound to many like genocide and ethnic cleansing.
2. This challenge needs an answer—not just for critics, but also because some passages in the Old Testament give even believers pause. What is going on here?

B. Remember what I said reading Scripture accurately requires:
1. To get a correct understanding of a passage, we need to be clear on . . .
   a. The context of the text or passage
   b. The purpose of the writing in the historical and cultural setting of its audience
   c. And the normal conventions of language of the readers
2. Each of these is necessary to make sense of passages like the ones above.

C. First, the language
1. It's common for writers to use dramatic and colorful language to press a point (think of a newspaper's sports page). The practice is not unique to our era, though. It goes back to ancient times.
2. Ancient Near Eastern military narrative commonly traded in hyperbole—exaggeration for the sake of emphasis—especially when it came to military conquest.[8]

---

8. For more detail, see Paul Copan, *Is God a Moral Monster? Making Sense of the Old Testament God* (Grand Rapids: Baker, 2011).

a. The practice is evident throughout battle reports of the time, and we find it in the Bible, as well.
   b. Simply put, the hyperbolic language of "utterly destroy" meant to "thoroughly defeat," not to "completely annihilate."
3. So, the first qualifier is that the wording of the conquest was not meant to be taken literally. Rather, it was exaggerated military metaphor—a common convention for ancient Near Eastern warfare accounts.
4. Here's how I might employ that insight in a dialogue:

   "The God of the Bible ordered genocide."
   > "Why do you say that?"

   "He told Joshua to annihilate every man, woman, and child of the Canaanites."
   > "Let me ask you a question: Do you ever read the sports page?"

   "Sure."
   > "Does it bother you when you read that one team completely wiped out another team?"

   "Of course not. They don't mean that literally."
   > "Well, God didn't mean that literally, either."

   "What?!"
   > "No, it's a figure of speech, just like sportswriters use. It was common in the records of ancient Near Eastern warfare, just like on the sports page. It's called 'military hyperbole.'"

   "Are you saying there was no conquest?"
   > "No, there were battles, and lots of people died. But there was no command to literally annihilate everyone."

   "How do you know that?"
   > "Because it's clear when you read the record more closely that it's not what the Israelites were commanded to do, nor was it what they did."

5. Now another point:
   a. Hyperbole, like all figurative speech, is meant to make a literal point.

b. God clearly wanted the Israelites to utterly defeat the Canaanites and drive them out.[9] Why?

   c. Two related issues are in play here, both tied to the historical/cultural setting.

D. Reaping the whirlwind

   1. First, a major purpose of the conquest was God's judgment on a despicable people for their wickedness:

   > When you enter the land which the LORD your God gives you, you shall not learn to imitate the detestable things of those nations. . . . Because of these detestable things the LORD your God will drive them out before you. (Deut. 18:9, 12)

   > It is because of the wickedness of these nations that the LORD your God is driving them out before you. (Deut. 9:5)

   2. God was angry. Indeed, he was furious. And with good reason.
   3. The Canaanites were unspeakably evil.
      a. In addition to divination, witchcraft, and all kinds of sexual debauchery, the Canaanites also practiced child sacrifice.

▎ Reflect a Moment

"Molech was a Canaanite underworld deity represented as an upright, bull-headed idol with human body in whose belly a fire was stoked and in whose outstretched arms a child was placed that would be burned to death. . . . And it was not just infants; children as old as four were sacrificed."[10]

      b. Sometimes the children that were sacrificed numbered in the thousands.
      c. The Canaanites reveled in debasements like these for centuries.

---

9. In Acts 7:45, Stephen referred to God *driving out* the nations and *dispossessing* them, not annihilating them.
10. Clay Jones, "We Don't Hate Sin, So We Don't Understand What Happened to the Canaanites: An Addendum to 'Divine Genocide' Arguments," *Philosophia Christi* 11, no. 1 (2009): 61, ibs.cru.org/files/5214/3336/7724/We-Dont-Hate-Sin-PC-article.pdf.

E. **Genocide or ethnic cleansing?**
   1. God didn't care about ethnicity.[11] God cared only about sin. These people deserved judgment.
   2. The conquest was neither ethnic cleansing nor genocide.
      a. It was an exercise of capital punishment on a national scale.
      b. In fact, God brought the same sentence on his own people when they did the same thing.[12]

▶ Reflect a Moment

What would atheists say if God perpetually sat silent in the face of such wickedness? Would they not ask, "Where was God?" Would they not question his goodness, his power, or even his existence if he didn't eventually vanquish this evil? Yet, when God finally does act, critics are quick to find fault with the "vindictive, bloodthirsty, ethnic cleanser."[13]

So first, God was punishing evil. But there was a second purpose for God's judgment.

F. **Cleaning house**
   1. God was purging the country of every trace of the evil Canaanite religion.
   2. He did not want his own people polluted by that wickedness.
      a. Unfortunately, the Hebrews soon did all the detestable things God had condemned Canaan for.[14]
      b. Eventually they got the same punishment for the same reasons.
         (1) Military destruction and expulsion from the land
         (2) For debauchery, idolatry, and child sacrifice
   3. Yes, the wording in God's commands about the conquest included exaggeration.
      a. But literary devices are always meant to clarify meaning.
      b. The clear message here is that God punishes evil.
   4. Here's another sample conversation on that issue:

---

11. Aliens—that is, foreigners living in the land—shared the same legal rights in the commonwealth as the Jews did (Lev. 19:34; 24:22; Deut. 10:18–19).
12. 1 Kings 9:7–9.
13. Richard Dawkins, *The God Delusion* (Boston: Houghton Mifflin, 2006), 31.
14. 2 Kings 17:16–18.

"There's another thing maybe you haven't thought about."

"What's that?"

"If you knew that religious groups were molesting massive numbers of children and even ritualistically burning them alive, what would you think about God?"

"I'd reject the whole idea of God."

"Why?"

"Because if a good God really existed, he'd do something about that."

"So, if something like that actually happened, you think God should step in?"

"Of course."

"So now the next question: Do you know the kinds of things the Canaanites did routinely?"

"No."

"They sexually abused children and ritually sacrificed infants, burning them alive. You asked me, if God existed, why wouldn't he do something?"

"Yes."

"God *did* do something. After waiting patiently for hundreds of years, he finally brought judgment on those people. Do you know what God did to the Israelites when they sacrificed their own children to idols?"

"No."

"He did the same thing to them that he did to the Canaanites. He drove them out of the land."

Now let's talk about a different volatile biblical issue: slavery.

IV. "Am I Not a Man and a Brother?"[15]

A. Slavery is one of the most misunderstood subjects in the Bible. There's a reason for this confusion.

---

15. These words adorned an emblem with an image of a black slave in chains. It was used as a symbol in the fight to abolish slavery.

1. Language, translation, and the historical context of the ancient Near East are completely foreign to twenty-first-century readers.
2. Instead, a different historical context now informs our understanding of the word *slave*.

B. When Americans read the word *slave* in the Bible, a vivid picture comes to mind.
1. It's an image of kidnapping, murder, rape, brutal forced servitude, disregard for basic human dignity, and complete lack of legal protection.
2. That's what we think of now when we see the word *slave* in Scripture.
3. That was the American system, a wretched practice that was finally abolished principally because of Christians.[16]

C. I want you to be clear on three details in the Mosaic law that must inform our understanding of "slavery" in the Bible.
1. First, kidnapping was a capital crime (Ex. 21:16).[17]
2. Second, murder was a capital crime (Gen. 9:6; Ex. 21:12). This prohibition explicitly included the killing of slaves (cf. Ex. 21:20).[18]
3. Third, rape was a capital crime (Deut. 22:25).
4. These facts alone are enough to show that the so-called slavery regulated in Old Testament law bore no resemblance to the kind of slavery we picture when Americans read that word.

There is another issue, though.

D. Lost in translation
1. Most people don't know that in their modern translations the words "slave" and "servant" are usually translated from the *same* Hebrew word: *ebed*.

---

16. England's William Wilberforce comes to mind, but there were many others.
17. Note also 1 Timothy 1:9–10: "Law is not made for a righteous person, but for those who are lawless and rebellious, for the ungodly and sinners, for . . . kidnappers . . . and whatever else is contrary to sound teaching."
18. In context, the punishment required in verse 20 would be the penalty described in verse 12: death.

2. Frequently, the preferred meaning of *ebed* is not slave, but "servant," even when the word *slave* appears in your translation.

   a. You can tell from the context (remember our rule: never read a Bible verse).

   b. The word refers principally to work and service, not to property and ownership.

▌Reflect a Moment

In my *Young's Analytical Concordance to the Bible*—published in 1897 and keyed to the King James Version—there is not a single instance where *ebed* was translated "slave." Instead, the KJV rendered *ebed* "bondman" 20 times, "manservant" 23 times, and "servant" 716 times. By the middle of the twentieth century, though, the trend had changed drastically.[19] My *New American Standard Exhaustive Concordance of the Bible* published in 1981, for example, reveals 58 instances when *ebed* is translated into some form of the word *slave*. Even so, in 722 instances, *ebed* is still rendered "servant" of some sort. Why the shift? I have no idea. Regardless of this unusual trend, it's clear that the preferred meaning of *ebed* is not slave, but servant.

E. **Why do we see "slavery" sanctioned in the Mosaic law?**

   1. To answer that question, we need to read these texts with the cultural eyes of the original audience.

   2. Keep in mind that in the ancient Near East, virtually everyone was an *ebed*—a servant or "slave"—of some sort.[20]

      a. Workers in the fields were servants of the landowners.

      b. Landowners were servants of their king.

      c. The king was servant to his God.

   3. Also, the ancient Near East in general was a world of brutal subjugation of other human beings.

   4. Because the Hebrews were apt to adopt those ways, God used the Law to place boundaries and controls to humanize some practices that were less than ideal.

---

19. I was alerted to this trend by Cambridge's Peter J. Williams.
20. See Dr. Peter J. Williams, "Lecture—Peter Williams 'Does the Bible Support Slavery?'" Lanier Library Lecture Series (Houston: Lanier Theological Library Chapel House, October 30, 2015), video shared by fleetwd1, December 2, 2015, on YouTube, youtube.com/watch?v=EUOsBQYuZ9g.

F. Help wanted

1. "Hiring out" as an *ebed* was a normal means of employment.
    a. Today we'd call that an "indentured servant."
    b. People in debt or without a job could lease out their labor by pledging themselves as workers.[21]
    c. Often, the ability to do that ensured a person's survival.
2. To protect the worker, though, God set clear boundaries and gave precise rights and protections to every *ebed* in the commonwealth.
3. In a sense, then, an *ebed* in ancient Israel had union representation: the Mosaic law. For example:
    a. Violence against an *ebed* was strictly forbidden.
    b. Every *ebed* had a day of Sabbath rest, just like everyone else.
    c. In the seventh year, every Israelite *ebed* was set free.
    d. A runaway *ebed* who escaped his master was not to be mistreated, but rather protected.
4. Here's a sample dialogue on that issue:

"The Old Testament condones slavery."

"When you hear the word 'slavery,' what picture comes to mind?"

"Africans in chains kidnapped and shipped to plantations for forced labor, being beaten, raped, and murdered at will."

"Is this what you think the Bible approves of?"

"Absolutely."

"If that were what it meant, I'd be angry, too. Did you know, though, that in the Mosaic law kidnapping was a capital crime punished by execution, and so were rape and murder?"

"I didn't know that."

"Is it possible, then, that the so-called slavery in the Old Testament was different from the slavery you just described?"

"I hadn't thought of that."

---

21. A father could even "sell" his daughter into servanthood to make provision for her long-term well-being (Ex. 21:7).

"Do you know the difference between the Hebrew word translated 'slave' in our modern translations and the Hebrew word translated 'servant'?"

"No."

"There is no difference. It's the exact same Hebrew word."

"Really?"

"Yep. Most of the time the word appears, it's talking about what we call indentured servants, not slaves—people who 'sell' themselves to work for someone else for a period of time. By the way, did African slaves in America have any rights?"

"Of course not."

"Well, the 'slaves' of the Jews did. They had every Saturday off, for example. And if you so much as broke a tooth of a slave, you had to set him free. One last thing."

"What's that?"

"Any idea how the ugly slavery we all abhor was finally abolished in the West?"

"Not exactly."

"Christians in England and in America ended it. Here's why: they were convinced from the Bible that slavery was a terrible sin against God."

5. My summary here doesn't cover every reference to servanthood/slavery in the Old Testament.[22]

6. Also, some of the laws regarding Hebrew servants did not apply in the same way to foreigners.

7. Nevertheless, the "slavery" under the Mosaic law bore no resemblance to the brutal practice of slavery in North America.

---

22. For a thorough treatment of the biblical texts on slavery, see Paul Copan, *Is God a Moral Monster? Making Sense of the Old Testament God* (Grand Rapids: Zondervan, 2011). See also Paul Copan, *Is God a Vindictive Bully? Reconciling Portrayals of God in the Old and New Testaments* (Grand Rapids: Baker Academic, 2022).

V. What Main Points Did We Cover in This Session?

A. First, I suggested—for strategic reasons—that in evangelism you not argue for the inerrancy of God's Word. You'll just get showered with charges of alleged contradictions.
  1. Instead, focus on the Bible as a reliable historical account of Jesus' life.
  2. That's the way most first-century people heard the gospel anyway—as a testimony of Jesus and his resurrection.

B. Second, I offered the single most important tip for reading your Bible accurately:
  1. Never read a Bible verse.
  2. Always read the larger context to get the flow of thought.

C. Next, we learned two things about the conquest of Canaan.
  1. First, it was customary in ancient Near Eastern warfare accounts to use hyperbole to exaggerate the details of military conquest. For example, "wipe out" meant to "utterly defeat," not to "completely annihilate."
  2. Second, God's principal goal was to judge the Canaanites for radical debauchery—including child sacrifice—and drive them out, purging the land of their despicable religion.
  3. God's command wasn't for genocide. It was a proper act of judgment by God on wicked people.

D. Finally, I made some important clarifications about "slavery" in the Bible.
  1. First, the so-called slavery regulated by Old Testament law bore no resemblance to the kind of slavery in America.
  2. Second, the Hebrew word *ebed*, translated "slave," also meant "servant" and, in the context, usually did.
  3. Third, many people "hired out" as *ebeds*—indentured servants—as a form of employment to protect them from poverty.

4. Finally, we learned that through the Mosaic law, God placed boundaries and controls on servanthood and slavery to humanize practices that were often less than ideal.

Self-Assessment

Try to answer the following questions without using your notes.

1. On strategic grounds, why is it a good idea not to argue with nonbelievers that the Bible is the inerrant Word of God?
   > If we make the claim that the Bible is God's inerrant Word, that often triggers an avalanche of _____ or claims about apparent _____ or _____.

2. What is a better strategy when using Scripture with nonbelievers?
   > A better strategy is to make our case based on the historical _____ of the Gospels, not on their divine _____.

3. What is the single most important principle to keep in mind when seeking to read the Bible accurately?
   > That single most important principle is "Never _____ a Bible _____."

4. To understand the meaning of any text we need to be clear on three things. What are they?
   > One, the flow of thought of the passage (its _____); two, the _____ it was written for (its historical/cultural _____); three, the normal conventions of _____ of that audience.

5. What's an important language element to keep in mind when reading Old Testament commands regarding the conquest of the land?
   > Ancient Near Eastern military narrative commonly used _____, which is _____ for the sake of emphasis. Language like "utterly destroy" meant "thoroughly defeat," not "completely _____."

6. List one of God's major purposes for the conquest of the land.

> God was bringing _____ on the Canaanites for their _____.

7. Name one serious act of evil the Canaanites practiced regularly that brought God's judgment.
   > The Canaanites practiced child _____.

8. Name a second major purpose for the conquest.
   > God was _____ the country of every trace of the evil Canaanite _____.

9. Give three indications from the Mosaic law showing that the "slavery" in the commonwealth of Israel was very different from slavery in America.
   > First, _____ was a capital crime. Second, _____ was a capital crime. Third, _____ was a capital crime.

10. What is the Hebrew word translated "slave," and what is unique about it?
    > The Hebrew word translated "slave" is _____, and it is the same word that is translated "_____."

11. What kind of "slave" is the Old Testament commonly referring to?
    > The word translated "slave" is frequently referring to what now would be called an indentured _____. It was a standard means of _____.

12. How did the Mosaic law protect the Jews from falling prey to abusive practices toward servants evident elsewhere in ancient Near Eastern culture?
    > The Mosaic law placed _____ boundaries on master/servant relationships and gave *ebeds* specific _____ and _____.

✓ Self-Assessment with Answers

1. If we make the claim that the Bible is God's inerrant Word, that often triggers an avalanche of **allegations** or claims about apparent **contradictions** or **discrepancies**.
2. A better strategy is to make our case based on the historical **reliability** of the Gospels, not on their divine **inspiration/inerrancy**.

3. That single most important principle is "Never **read** a Bible **verse**."
4. One, the flow of thought of the passage (its **context**); two, the **audience** it was written for (its historical/cultural **setting**); three, the normal conventions of **language** of that audience.
5. Ancient Near Eastern military narrative commonly used **hyperbole**, which is **exaggeration** for the sake of emphasis. Language like "utterly destroy" meant "thoroughly defeat," not "completely **annihilate**."
6. God was bringing **judgment** on the Canaanites for their **wickedness**.
7. The Canaanites practiced child **sacrifice**.
8. God was **cleansing** the country of every trace of the evil Canaanite **religion**.
9. First, **kidnapping** was a capital crime. Second, **murder** was a capital crime. Third, **rape** was a capital crime.
10. The Hebrew word translated "slave" is *ebed*, and it is the same word that is translated "**servant**."
11. The word translated "slave" is frequently referring to what now would be called an indentured **servant**. It was a standard means of **employment**.
12. The Mosaic law placed **protective** boundaries on master/servant relationships and gave *ebeds* specific **rights** and **privileges**.

Interactive Group Study Questions

1. Discuss why it is better to build our case for Christianity on the historical reliability of the Bible rather than on inerrancy, even though we're convinced Scripture is inerrant.
2. Talk about what Greg means when he advises people to "Never read a Bible verse."
3. Discuss how you might answer the charge that the God of the Old Testament was patently immoral? How does a proper reading of Scripture help us understand and answer this challenge?
4. How does the illustration of hyperbole in a sports story in the newspaper give us a more accurate understanding of the dramatic language used to describe military conquests in the Bible?
5. Talk about the images that come to mind when you read the word *slave* in the Bible. How is this picture different from the "slavery" sanctioned in the Law? Discuss the details in the Mosaic law that support your view.

6. What are some of the ways God set clear boundaries that gave precise rights and protections to every *ebed* in Israel?

Going Deeper: Information for Self-Study

Explain to a friend the things you've covered in this lesson.

1. Explain the single most important tip for reading the Bible and why it's important.
2. Share with your friend the most important details to keep in mind when reading about the Hebrews' conquest of Canaan.
3. Finally, provide some insight on how the Hebrew word *ebed* applies to the issue of slavery in the Bible, and then share some of the things God included in the Law to protect poor people in ancient Israel.
4. Be prepared to share your experiences with the group when you get together next time.

Food for Thought

Very Nasty People

In addition to divination, witchcraft, and female and male temple sex, Canaanite idolatry encompassed a host of morally detestable practices that mimicked the sexually perverse conduct of their Canaanite fertility gods:[23] adultery, homosexuality, transvestitism, pederasty (men sexually abusing boys), sex with all sorts of beasts,[24] and incest. Note that after the Canaanite city of Sodom was destroyed, Lot's daughters immediately seduced their drunken father, imitating one of the sexual practices of the city just annihilated (Gen. 19:30–36).

A Book of Books

Note that the Bible is not a single book, but a "library" of books that were circulating individually around the Mediterranean in the first century. Later—in the second century and beyond—they were bound together under one cover (a codex), creating the volume we call the Bible.

---

23. Canaanite fertility religion tied eroticism of all sorts to the successful cycles of planting and harvest.
24. This may explain God's command to destroy even domestic animals in some cases.

GOD: THE SCIENCE STOPPER?

⬜ Demonstrating Mastery

Try recalling the answers to the following questions without using your notes. The answers are in the "Self-Assessment with Answers" section of session 7.

1. What is the single most important principle to keep in mind when seeking to read the Bible accurately?
2. To understand the meaning of any text we need to be clear on three things. What are they?
3. What is the Hebrew word translated "slave," and what is unique about it?
4. What kind of "slave" is the Old Testament commonly referring to?

I. Review and Looking Ahead

A. In the preceding session, we covered the following:
  1. First, I suggested—for strategic reasons—that in evangelism you not argue for the inerrancy of God's Word. You'll just get showered with charges of alleged contradictions.
     a. Instead, focus on the Bible as a reliable historical account of Jesus' life.
     b. That's the way most first-century people heard the gospel anyway—as a testimony of Jesus and his resurrection.

2. Second, I offered the single most important tip for reading your Bible accurately:
   a. Never read a Bible verse.
   b. Always read the larger context to get the flow of thought.
3. Next, we learned two things about the conquest of Canaan.
   a. First, it was customary in ancient Near Eastern warfare accounts to use hyperbole to exaggerate the details of military conquest. For example, "wipe out" meant to "utterly defeat," not to "completely annihilate."
   b. Second, God's principal goal was to judge the Canaanites for radical debauchery—including child sacrifice—and drive them out, purging the land of their despicable religion.
   c. God's command wasn't for genocide. It was a proper act of judgment by God on wicked people.
4. Finally, I made some important clarifications about "slavery" in the Bible.
   a. First, the so-called slavery regulated by Old Testament law bore no resemblance to the kind of slavery in America.
   b. Second, the Hebrew word *ebed*, translated "slave," also meant "servant" and, in the context, usually did.
   c. Third, many people "hired out" as *ebeds*—indentured servants—as a form of employment to protect them from poverty.
   d. Finally, we learned that through the Mosaic law, God placed boundaries and controls on servanthood and slavery to humanize practices that were often less than ideal.

B. In this session, we'll cover the alleged conflict between science and religion.
   1. First, I want you to see that it's not possible for science to disprove God or miracles or souls or anything like that, because that task is completely beyond its capability.
   2. Second, the alleged "conflict" between science and religion is completely contrived.
      a. Science and Christian religion, at least, are not inherently at odds.
      b. Rather, the battle between science and religion has been a not-so-subtle philosophical power play designed to keep the God alternative off the table.

3. Third, I want you to see why in certain important cases appealing to God as an explanation is not a "God of the gaps" error.
4. Finally, I'll show you that historically, belief in God wasn't a science stopper but a science starter—and for good reason.

II. Sleight of Hand

A. **For over a hundred years, people have used science as a stick to beat up on religion.**
   1. For them, any claims that are not in principle provable by science must be contrary to science, and if contrary to science, then irrational.
      a. Supernatural events can't be explained by science and natural law.
      b. Therefore, no religious claims—especially miracles—can be taken seriously by anyone serious about science and reason.
   2. In the minds of many, then, science has weighed in with finality against God. They used to believe in God, but now they believe in science.
   3. Worse, any appeal to God as a causal agent—the so-called God of the gaps move—is a science stopper.

B. **What I want to show you is . . .**
   1. A philosophic sleight of hand is in play here.
   2. Once you see the maneuver, you will not be fooled by the con.

III. Weighing a Chicken with a Yardstick

A. **Let me start by asking what might seem like an odd question: Can you weigh a chicken with a yardstick?**
   1. Of course not. Yardsticks measure length, not weight.
   2. Does it follow, then, that chickens have no weight?

3. Again, no. Tools meant to measure one feature tell you nothing about other features they can't measure.

B. This notion is so basic that it's easy to miss its significance when it comes to the question of science and the supernatural, so let me state it bluntly.

1. Strictly speaking, science is not capable of ruling out anything—even in principle—about the immaterial realm.
2. Science is designed to measure physical things using empirical methods.
    a. That means it's only capable of drawing conclusions about the physical things it measures, not about anything nonphysical it can't measure.
    b. This is not a criticism of science but rather a levelheaded acknowledgment of the natural limitations of the method. That's all.

C. Confusion and error result when someone assumes that if science can't measure it, then it doesn't exist.

1. For example, years ago *Time* magazine featured an article on consciousness.
2. In the article's conclusion, the writers admitted they didn't know what consciousness *was*, but they were convinced they knew what consciousness *was not*:

> Despite our every instinct to the contrary, there is one thing that consciousness is not: some entity deep inside the brain that corresponds to the "self," some kernel of awareness that runs the show.[1]

3. How do they know that?

> After more than a century of looking for it, brain researchers have long since concluded that there is no conceivable place for such a self to be located in the physical brain, and that it simply doesn't exist.[2]

---

1. Michael D. Lemonick, "Glimpses of the Mind," *Time*, July 17, 1995, 52, content.time.com/time/subscriber/article/0,33009,983176-8,00.html.
2. Ibid.

4. In other words, scientists say souls don't exist because:
    a. They can't find it by looking for it, and . . .
    b. There is no room in the brain for it to fit.
5. That's like saying, "You said there was an invisible man in your house, but I looked inside and didn't see him anywhere."
    a. Scientists are not going to find an immaterial soul by looking for it even if they search for a hundred years since no one can see something that's invisible.
    b. Plus, immaterial things like souls don't need physical places to "fit" into. Immaterial objects, by nature, do not occupy three-dimensional space.
6. This doesn't prove souls exist, of course.
    a. It does show, though, that the inability of science to find one means nothing.
    b. The question of the existence of the soul must be resolved in a different way.

D. Please do not miss this critical point.
1. Science can help us in many ways.
2. However, it cannot foreclose on anything—souls, spirits, God(s), salvation, heaven, hell—outside its domain for a simple reason: it is not equipped to measure those things. It's like trying to weigh a chicken with a yardstick.
3. This approach to defeating theism is a dead end.
4. Here's a sample conversation that makes this point:

> "I used to believe in God, but now I believe in science."
>> "Explain that to me. I'm not sure I understand what the conflict is." [Columbo #1]
>
> "You know, I used to believe in all that supernatural stuff, but science has shown me none of that is real."
>> "Can you help me understand exactly how science has shown the supernatural can't be real?"
>
> "Well, ancient people used to believe lots of things, like weather, were caused by gods. Now from science we know the real reason for weather, and it has nothing to do with gods."

"I agree. There are lots of ways science has cleared up confusion for us, but you're saying something different, aren't you?"

"What's that?"

"Well, you're saying that science has somehow shown that the supernatural world is not real. I'm just asking how science can do that."

"I guess I don't get your point."

"Science studies the physical world, right?"

"Right."

"It studies things you can know through your five senses, correct?"

"Correct."

"If there really were immaterial things like gods or souls or spirits or miraculous powers, would any of those things be physical?"

"Of course not."

"Well, if they wouldn't be physical, how can science have anything to say about them? How can an empirical way of knowing show that nonempirical things don't exist?"

Reflect a Moment

Here's the problem: science has never advanced empirical evidence showing that supernatural events can't happen. Instead, it has *assumed*—prior to the evidence[3]—that the material world is all there is. That's not science. That's philosophy.

IV. A Stacked Deck

A. **The most popular science documentary of all time starts with these words: "The cosmos is all that is, or ever was, or ever will be."**

   1. The film is PBS's *Cosmos: A Personal Voyage*, hosted by legendary astronomer Carl Sagan.[4]

---

3. This kind of assumption is called an *a priori* belief—one that is alleged prior to and apart from observation or experience.
4. *Cosmos: A Personal Voyage*, episode 1, "The Shores of the Cosmic Ocean," 4:27.

God: The Science Stopper? ▪ 159

        a. Oddly, the opening line of the documentary is not scientific at all. No empirical analysis can ever reveal "all that is, or ever was, or ever will be"—even in principle.

        b. No, Sagan's famous words are pure materialistic, naturalistic philosophy.

  2. Sagan's starting point is not a *conclusion* of science. Rather, it's a philosophical presumption *imposed* on the scientific project.

  3. What's that presumption?

        a. The physical universe is all there is.

        b. Therefore, science is the best way—some think the *only* way—to gain reliable knowledge about reality.

B. The assumption expressed so memorably in *Cosmos* is what has artificially put science at odds with religion.

  1. For example, consider this statement by an atheist: "There's no resurrection because I know from science that dead people stay dead."[5]

        a. Science, of course, teaches no such thing.

        b. Science can tell us if a body is dead or if it's alive.

        c. It cannot tell us if a dead body can be raised to life again or not. It is not science that tells the atheist that resurrections can't happen. His philosophy dictates that.

💬 Reflect a Moment

The world we live in may be a purely physical place run entirely by natural law, no exceptions. Or the world may be possessed of powers beyond mere physical cause and effect. In that kind of world, resurrections are plausible. The critical question is this: What kind of world do we live in? Science is mute on that matter. That question is one for philosophers, not scientists.

  2. I said above that this philosophical move pitting science against religion is no accident but is a conscious and deliberate contrivance.

---

5. Natasha Crain, *Faithfully Different: Regaining Biblical Clarity in a Secular Culture* (Eugene, OR: Harvest House, 2022), 69.

3. To verify this point, let me read a striking statement made by a world-class geneticist at Harvard—Richard Lewontin—who, without shame or embarrassment, admits the science game has been rigged:

> Our willingness to accept scientific claims that are against common sense is the key to an understanding of the real struggle between science and the supernatural. We take the side of science *in spite of* the patent absurdity of some of its constructs . . . because we have a prior commitment, a commitment to materialism. . . . We are forced by our . . . adherence to material causes to create an apparatus of investigation, and a set of concepts, that produce material explanations, no matter how counter-intuitive, no matter how mystifying to the uninitiated. . . . Moreover, that materialism is absolute, for we cannot allow a Divine Foot in the door.[6]

4. Richard Lewontin is not the only one to make such an admission, but he is undoubtedly the most brazen, which is why he is cited so frequently.[7]

Reflect a Moment

Phillip Johnson, founding father of the intelligent design movement, sums up Lewontin's point well: "The reason for opposition to scientific accounts of our origins, according to Lewontin, is not that people are ignorant of facts, but that they have not learned to think from the right starting point."[8]

5. Here is the consequence.
   a. Intelligent design is uniformly disqualified as being "unscientific."
   b. It is not rejected based on its evidential merits—that reasonable evidence for intelligent design is lacking. Rather, it is rejected on its philosophic implications—its violation of materialist philosophy.
6. Here's a way these points might play out in conversation:

---

6. Richard Lewontin, "Billions and Billions of Demons," *New York Review*, January 9, 1997, www.nybooks.com/articles/1997/01/09/billions-and-billions-of-demons/, emphasis in the original.
7. I quote Lewontin and discuss this issue at length in chapter 15 of my book *Tactics*.
8. Phillip E. Johnson, "The Unraveling of Scientific Materialism," *First Things*, November 1997, www.firstthings.com/article/1997/11/the-unraveling-of-scientific-materialism.

"Intelligent design is not science. It's religion disguised as science."

"Really? How so?" [Columbo #1]

"Science is all about physical events, empirically verified. Intelligent design brings God into the picture. That's not science."

"So, you're objecting because theists suggest that some agent, not some physical cause, is responsible for certain features of the natural world?" [Columbo #1]

"Exactly."

"Is archaeology science?"

"Of course."

"Doesn't archeology study the role of agents in history?"

"Sure."

"What about forensic pathology?"

"Of course, but those are different."

"Why?"

"They're human agents, not supernatural ones."

"But what if the evidence is really good that a supernatural agent is the best explanation of certain physical facts?"

"It's still religion, not science."

"I have another question about that."

"Okay."

"It sounds like you're rejecting intelligent design because, strictly speaking according to your definition, it's religious."

"Right."

"Usually when an option is rejected, it's not because it's a certain category of answer—like 'religious'—but because it's based on bad facts or unsound thinking. So, what are the specific reasons you don't think intelligent design is a good explanation for, say, the origin of life or the information in DNA?"

Now another objection: appealing to supernatural explanations is just the "God of the gaps" fallacy.

V. God of the Gaps?

A. Here's the critic's claim: just because science hasn't solved some of the problems, that doesn't mean it never will.
1. There's no need to punt to superstition (that is, religion).
2. A rational (that is, naturalistic) answer will eventually be available.
3. Using God to arbitrarily plug holes that science hasn't filled yet is misguided.

B. Here's my response:[9]
1. First, this complaint is circular. It *assumes* as part of its argument what needs to be *proved* by the argument.
   a. The charge presumes there will always be a naturalistic explanation.
      (1) Why? Because naturalism is true, so science is bound to solve the problem eventually.
      (2) Of course, the whole point at issue is whether naturalism is true or not.
   b. All this objection does is replace the so-called God of the gaps with a "naturalism of the gaps."
   c. The real issue is this: All prejudices aside, which explanation best fits the evidence?

▶ Reflect a Moment

Why assume there's a "gap" in our knowledge simply because we have no explanations consistent with materialism? It's possible that some breaches remain because we've been slavishly looking for answers in the wrong place.

2. Second, careful appeals to a supernatural agent (God) are not based on ignorance.
   a. Appealing to a divine designer isn't a leap of faith based on what we *don't* know.
   b. The appeal is a conclusion based on what we *do* know.
      (1) Design can be detected empirically.
      (2) If the evidence is good for design, then there's no gap.

---

9. For a thorough treatment of the God of the gaps question, see Stephen C. Meyer, *Return of the God Hypothesis* (New York: HarperCollins, 2021), ch. 20.

(3) It has been filled with a real answer based on good reasons.
   c. Just because the solution is not the right *kind* of answer for some—a naturalistic one—doesn't mean it's not the *right* answer.
3. Third, sometimes the very nature of an event makes a naturalistic explanation completely implausible.
   a. It may be theoretically possible that a man with five bullet holes in his chest died from natural causes, but that doesn't mean it's reasonable to hold out for a natural explanation.
   b. What really matters is the evidence at hand, not future fantasies.
4. Here's a sample dialogue:

"When you appeal to a supernatural cause, that's just the God of the gaps fallacy all over again.'

"What exactly is the problem here?"

"You see a gap in the scientific explanation, so you just say, 'God did it.'"

"Is that what you think I've been doing?"

"Yes."

"But what about the good evidence for a supernatural designer—like the origin of the universe or the origin of life or the incredible fine-tuning we see in the cosmos and in the biological world?"

"Science will eventually find the answers to those problems and fill the gap."

"Help me understand why that isn't an example of naturalism of the gaps."

"Well, science has shown it can answer the issues without any need for God."

"So, you're confident your naturalism of the gaps is okay, even though you don't have the evidence in this case, but God is not an okay answer, even though there's good evidence for a supernatural agent. Is that right?"

VI. God, the Science Starter

A. Religion and science have not always been in conflict. That is a recent development historically.

1. The warfare model is largely the result of two books from the late nineteenth century.
    a. *A History of the Conflict between Religion and Science* by John Draper in 1874
    b. *A History of the Warfare of Science with Theology in Christendom* by Andrew White in 1896
    c. Both works fanned the flames between evolutionists and religious fundamentalists, pitting—as the authors characterized it—science and progress against superstition and repression.
2. Historians of science, though, give a different account of the role religion played in the birth of modern science.
    a. Naturalism was not the driving force in the early days.
    b. Rather, theological conviction was a foundational factor in the genesis of science.

B. **The basic methods of science sprouted, ironically, from the theological soil of Christian Europe.[10] Here's why:**
1. The obvious order of nature fit the Christian convictions of the pioneers of modern science.
    a. It was clear to them that a divine mind had ordered the world.
    b. If a rational God fashioned the universe, then rational man—made in God's image—could unlock its secrets.
2. That was the thinking of men like astronomer Johannes Kepler, chemist Robert Boyle, and physicist Isaac Newton.
    a. In fact, Newton wrote more on theology than he did on science—1.3 million words.[11]
    b. These men viewed nature as God's second "book" of revelation.
3. They also understood that given the fall, human reason was fallible.
    a. Systematic testing, experimentation, and close observation were all necessary, then, to avoid error.
    b. The "scientific method" began to take shape.

---

10. For a fascinating account of the birth of science in the Western world, see Meyer, *Return of the God Hypothesis*, pt. 1.

11. According to Vincent Carroll and David Shiflett, *Christianity on Trial: Arguments against Anti-Religious Bigotry* (San Francisco: Encounter Books, 2002), 77.

C. Here's a partial list of deeply committed theists—all founders of their respective fields in science—whose religious convictions complemented rather than conflicted with their scientific efforts:
   1. Nicolaus Copernicus (b. 1473)—Polish mathematician and astronomer; established the foundation of modern astronomy by proposing the heliocentric theory of planetary motion
   2. Galileo Galilei (b. 1564)—Italian physicist and astronomer; empirically confirmed heliocentrism and pioneered the modern scientific method
   3. Johannes Kepler (b. 1571)—German astronomer; discovered the laws of planetary motion
   4. Blaise Pascal (b. 1623)—French mathematical prodigy; founded modern probability theory and hydraulics, and contributed to the advance of differential calculus
   5. Robert Boyle (b. 1627)—Irish developer of the modern scientific method; founder of modern chemistry
   6. Isaac Newton (b. 1642)—English mathematician, physicist, astronomer, and theologian; developed the principle of universal gravity
   7. Carolus Linnaeus (b. 1707)—Swedish botanist; founder of taxonomy, the modern scientific classification of plants and animals
   8. Georges Cuvier (b. 1769)—French naturalist; founded comparative anatomy; was father of paleontology
   9. Michael Faraday (b. 1791)—English physicist and chemist; discovered the principles of electromagnetic induction
   10. Gregor Mendel (b. 1822)—Augustinian monk; father of modern genetics

D. **One thing is clear from history:**
   1. There's never been any inherent hostility between the Christian worldview and the methods or principles of science proper. Christianity is not at war with science. It never has been.
   2. Rather, Western civilization—grounded in the biblical worldview—was the birthplace of the scientific enterprise. God was not a science stopper. He was the science starter.

Reflect a Moment

The uniformity of order these founding fathers of science observed in nature was a fingerprint of the Intelligent Designer who made the natural world that way. The mechanisms they observed in nature perfectly coincided with their conviction that a divine clockmaker had designed them.

E. **This doesn't prove the Christian views of these scientists were correct, of course. That's another project.**
  1. What it does show is that, for them, there was no inherent conflict between their Christian worldview and the methods of science they were developing.
  2. The conflict came when the philosophy of materialism was artificially imposed on the scientific enterprise, demanding the *right kind* of answers, not necessarily the *right* answers.
  3. Here's a sample dialogue that trades on these ideas:

> "Religion has always been at war with science."
>> "What exactly is the conflict?" [Columbo #1]
>
> "Religious people think faith is more important than reason."
>> "Do you know where modern science began?"
>
> "No."
>> "It began in Western Europe. Do you know why?"
>
> "I have no idea."
>> "Because they believed in a God who made an orderly world that could be discovered through careful observation."
>
> "I never heard that."
>> "Do you know who the founders of science were and what their beliefs were?"
>
> "Well, I know about people like Copernicus and Galileo. The church persecuted them because of their scientific beliefs."
>> "I understand that, but do you know what their own theological beliefs were?"
>
> "Not really."

"Those two were Christians, along with just about every other founding father of modern science."

"Really?"

"Really. In fact, Isaac Newton wrote more on theology than he did on science. He believed that what he discovered in science would help him understand God better. There was no conflict in Newton's mind between science and religion."

"So where did all this conflict come from?"

"It came because of a different religion."

"Really? Which one?"

"The religion of naturalism."

"Well, that's better than sticking God into the gap."

"Here's what I suggest. Why not just follow the evidence wherever it leads? Usually, we'll discover that the causes of natural events will be natural. No problem. Sometimes, though, the evidence points to an agent, like it does in forensic pathology. Sometimes it might even point to a supernatural agent. What's wrong with that?"

"Because that approach will kill science."

"Well, that's hard to believe since, historically, religion was the science starter. Let me suggest this, though. How about if we just use the methods of science to find out the truth about our world, whatever it is—no inquisitions on either side? What do you think?"

4. No discoveries of science have in any way compromised theism or belief in the supernatural.

5. In fact, what science has discovered about the universe in the last one hundred years has made the existence of a divine designer more probable, not less probable.

F. Here is the real issue:

1. Will the scientific community use its fine methodology to follow the truth wherever it leads, or . . .

2. Will it try to replay Galileo's inquisition in reverse and use law, politics, and intimidation to silence any opposition to its own modern creation story?

VII. What Main Points Did We Cover in This Session?

A. **First, I explained why it's not possible for science to disprove God or miracles or souls or anything of the sort.**
   1. That task is completely beyond its capability. It's like trying to weigh a chicken with a yardstick.
   2. Science cannot inveigh against anything it's not capable of measuring with empirical methods.

B. **Second, the alleged battle between science and religion has been a philosophical power play designed to keep the God option off the table.**
   1. Science is not currently defined simply by a fine methodology to give us the right answers about the universe.
   2. It is restrained by a philosophy—called *naturalism* or *materialism*—that also forces scientists give the right *kind* of answers.

C. **Third, appealing to God as an explanation for unique events in the universe is not an example of the "God of the gaps" fallacy.**
   1. First, the claim is circular since it presumes that naturalism is true—so naturalistic explanations will eventually fill all the explanatory gaps.
   2. Second, appeals to a designer are not based on ignorance, but on evidence. In many cases, then, there is no gap. An adequate, well-justified design explanation fills the so-called gap.

D. **Finally, history shows that belief in God was the science starter, not a science stopper—and for good reason.**
   1. Both the methods of science and much of the foundational content of science arose in Christian Western Europe.

2. The fathers of science saw the uniformity of order in nature and concluded a divine mind had ordered the world.
3. If a rational God fashioned the universe, then rational man made in the image of God could unlock its secrets through systematic testing, experimentation, and close observation.
4. Consequently, theists were founding figures in astronomy, physics, mathematics, taxonomy, chemistry, paleontology, electromagnetism, and genetics.

❓ Self-Assessment

Try to answer the following questions without using your notes.

1. Why is science not capable—even in principle—of ruling out the existence of anything in the immaterial realm?
   ▸ Science can't rule out the existence of anything in the immaterial realm because science is only capable of measuring _____ things using _____ methods.

2. Why is it odd for someone to say that souls don't exist because there's no scientific evidence for them?
   ▸ If souls do exist, they are _____ and do not extend in space. Therefore, it will not be possible to find or detect them with _____ methods. Failure to scientifically detect souls tells us _____ about the existence or nonexistence of souls.

3. Why is it ironic that the most popular science documentary of all time starts with the words "The cosmos is all that is, or ever was, or ever will be"?
   ▸ The reason this statement is ironic is that nothing about it is a conclusion of _____. Instead, it's simply an unproven _____ of _____ philosophy.

4. In what sense is the conflict between science and religion contrived?
   ▸ The conflict is contrived because modern science is not committed to finding the right _____ by following the _____ wherever it leads, but rather finding the right _____ of answers—answers that are consistent with the philosophy of

_____. The conflict is not between science and religion, but between _____ philosophy and _____ philosophy.

5. What are three problems with the "God of the gaps" complaint against intelligent design?
   > First, the charge is _____ because it assumes _____ is true and there will always be a _____ explanation eventually. This is nothing more than naturalism of the _____. Two, the appeals being made to a supernatural agent are not based on _____, but on _____. Three, for certain events—for example, the origin of the universe, the origin of life, and the DNA genetic code— _____ explanations are completely _____.

6. Why did the basic methods of science emerge from Western Europe?
   > Western Europe was the birthplace of modern science because those first scientists were convinced that a divine _____ had made an _____ world and that humans made in God's _____ could discover nature's secrets.

7. What is a good reply to the claim that appeals to God will be a science stopper?
   > With the origins of science, God was not a science _____. He was the science _____.

✓ Self-Assessment with Answers

1. Science can't rule out the existence of anything in the immaterial realm because science is only capable of measuring **physical** things using **empirical** methods.
2. If souls do exist, they are **immaterial** and do not extend in space. Therefore, it will not be possible to find or detect them with **scientific** methods. Failure to scientifically detect souls tells us **nothing** about the existence or nonexistence of souls.
3. The reason this statement is ironic is that nothing about it is a conclusion of **science**. Instead, it's simply an unproven **assertion** of **materialistic/naturalistic** philosophy.
4. The conflict is contrived because modern science is not committed to finding the right **answers** by following the **evidence** wherever it leads, but rather finding

the right **kind** of answers—answers that are consistent with the philosophy of **naturalism**. The conflict is not between science and religion, but between **materialistic** philosophy and **theistic** philosophy.

5. First, the charge is **circular** because it assumes **naturalism** is true and there will always be a **naturalistic** explanation eventually. This is nothing more than naturalism of the **gaps**. Two, the appeals being made to a supernatural agent are not based on **ignorance**, but on **evidence**. Three, for certain events—for example, the origin of the universe, the origin of life, and the DNA genetic code—**naturalistic** explanations are completely **implausible**.

6. Western Europe was the birthplace of modern science because those first scientists were convinced that a divine **mind** had made an **orderly** world and that humans made in God's **image** could discover nature's secrets.

7. With the origins of science, God was not a science **stopper**. He was the science **starter**.

Interactive Group Study Questions

1. Why do many people think science and faith are incompatible?
2. Discuss why the question "Can you weigh a chicken with a yardstick?" illustrates the problem with trying to explain away supernatural events using science and natural law.
3. What do we mean when we say that science is not capable of ruling out anything about the immaterial realm? Why is this not a criticism of science?
4. Discuss why Carl Sagan's famous phrase "The cosmos is all that is, or ever was, or ever will be" is unusual give the focus of "cosmos." What is the presumption here? How does Sagan's approach influence the science/faith discussion?
5. Critics claim that just because science hasn't solved some of the problems doesn't mean it never will. Discuss how this "naturalism of the gaps" explanation is circular reasoning.
6. Discuss what Christian convictions of the founders of modern science led to the development of the scientific method.
7. How did the alleged conflict between science and faith begin? Discuss why you think this misperception is so deeply ingrained in people's minds.

💡 Going Deeper: Information for Self-Study

Share with a friend the things you've covered in this lesson.

1. Explain to him why it's not possible for science to disprove God or rule out the possibility of miracles.
2. Help your friend understand the difference between the methods of science designed to give the right answers and the philosophy of materialism designed to give the right kind of answers.
3. Sketch out as best you can the reasons why modern science grew out of Christian theological convictions in Western Europe. Then give a few examples of the Christian founding fathers of various scientific disciplines.
4. Be prepared to share your experiences with the group when you get together next time.

Food for Thought

"Nothing Buttery"

In *Cosmos*, Carl Sagan offers a worldview story meant to compete with classic theism. Where the Christian story begins with the words "In the beginning, God," Carl Sagan's story begins, essentially, with the words "In the beginning, the particles."

Sagan's worldview is variously called *physicalism*, *materialism*, or *naturalism* since the basic concept is that reality consists of nothing but the physical, material world, governed by nothing but natural law.[12] Thus, C. S. Lewis called this the "nothing buttery" view.

Do not underestimate the power this presumption has to influence people's thinking about religion. For many you'll encounter, it's the philosophical air they breathe without realizing it. To them, the entire world is, from top to bottom, "nothing but" swirling atoms and molecules, in which "we float like a mote of dust in the morning sky," in Sagan's words from *Cosmos*.[13]

---

12. Sagan did not describe himself as atheist, though, but agnostic since he believed no one could be certain about God's existence. He was a deeply committed naturalist, however. Sagan here falls prey to the same knowledge/belief confusion I described in the "Food for Thought" section of session 4.

13. *Cosmos: A Personal Voyage*, episode 1, "The Shores of the Cosmic Ocean," 4:27.

Book, Clock, Law

The early scientists used three metaphors to convey their understanding of the natural world they were exploring: a *book*, a *clock*, and a realm governed by *law*.

These men viewed nature as God's second "book" of revelation, displaying what the apostle Paul described as God's "invisible attributes, His eternal power and divine nature."[14] The natural realm spoke with a "voice" that had gone out to all the earth.[15]

Clocks run mechanistically, reflecting the intelligence of a skillful clockmaker. The "clockwork universe" invited observers—if they were careful and methodical—to discover the specific physical mechanisms that made nature's clock "tick."

The mechanical regularity of nature coincided with the belief that some sort of governing force directed its behavior. "Law" language made perfect sense to those encountering the natural regularities. Even today, law terminology is the standard way of describing how the universe behaves.

Galileo Redux

Have there been genuine conflicts in the past between Christian authorities and the ideas of scientists? Of course. Galileo is a prime example. However, in Galileo's case—as is often the case today—some of the disagreement was on matters of scientific fact, not theology. Scientists disagree with each other all the time. Many opposed the heliocentric view on the merits, even though they were later proved wrong.

The challenge we face today is the same one Galileo faced. Then, the reigning *religious* powers resisted Galileo's science on philosophical grounds, not scientific ones, intimidating him into silence. Currently, the inquisition's boot is on the other foot, but the pattern is the same. Now, the reigning *scientific* powers silence opposition for philosophic reasons, not scientific ones. The dynamic is the very same one that corrupted science in the past.

---

14. Romans 1:20.
15. Romans 10:18; cf. Psalm 19:4.

SESSION 9

ABORTION: ONLY ONE QUESTION

Demonstrating Mastery

Try recalling the answers to the following questions without using your notes. The answers are in the "Self-Assessment with Answers" section of session 8.

1. Why is science not capable—even in principle—of ruling out the existence of anything in the immaterial realm?
2. What are three problems with the "God of the gaps" complaint against intelligent design?
3. What were the three metaphors the early scientists used to describe the natural world they were discovering?
4. What is a good reply to the claim that appeals to God will be a science stopper?

I. Review and Looking Ahead

A. In the preceding session, we covered the following:

1. First, I explained why it's not possible for science to disprove God or miracles or souls or anything of the sort.
2. Second, the alleged battle between science and religion has been a philosophical power play designed to keep the God option off the table.

3. Third, appealing to God as an explanation for unique events in the universe is not an example of the "God of the gaps" fallacy.
4. Finally, history shows that belief in God was the science starter, not a science stopper—and for good reason.

B. **Here is what we'll cover in this session:**
1. First, I'll share a strategy focusing on the single question that is the linchpin in the abortion debate, yet it's one almost no one talks about.
2. Second, I'll introduce the simple moral logic of the pro-life view.
3. Next, I'll show you why denying the personhood of the unborn is not a legitimate justification for abortion.
4. Fourth, I'll equip you to respond to the "my body, my choice" and the "right to refuse" challenges.
5. Next, I'll introduce you to the powerful "universal human rights" strategy against abortion.
6. Finally, I'll give you the most compelling scriptural argument against abortion.
7. Also, I've included a lot more sample conversations than usual here to make the important points clear for you.

C. **Let me introduce our next concern with a brief history lesson.**
1. On the morning of September 11, 2001, 2,977 innocent human beings were murdered when planes flown by Islamic terrorists crashed into three locations in the United States.
    a. This is something we're all familiar with, of course, but here's something you may not know. The number of humans murdered on 9/11 was less, on average, than the number of children who have died by abortion in America every single day for nearly half a century.
        (1) In the US alone, 63,459,781 abortions have been performed since *Roe v. Wade*—3,448 a day.[1]

---

1. National Right to Life, "Reported Annual Abortions 1973–2019," January 2022, nrlc.org/uploads/factsheets/FS01AbortionintheUS.pdf. Based on numbers reported by the pro-choice Guttmacher Institute, originally founded as a research arm of Planned Parenthood.

(2) That's 21,316 consecutive 9/11 days of death.
2. It took Hitler thirteen years to vaporize 6 million Jews. It took Americans six years after *Roe v. Wade* to beat Hitler through abortion. That's ten Holocausts back to back.
3. No moral issue, no political issue, no human rights issue has greater significance in the twenty-first century than abortion. The most dangerous place for a baby to be is resting in her mother's womb.

II. "Daddy, Can I Kill This?"

A. Here's the conversation I always open with to focus on the single most important issue in the abortion discussion.
1. I call this approach "Only One Question." That question is: What is the unborn?
2. Make this your first move, too.

> "Consider this analogy. Your child comes up behind you while you're working at some task and asks, 'Mommy/Daddy, can I kill this?' What is the one question you must ask before you can answer their question?"
>
> "I need to ask them, 'What is it?'"[2]
>
> "Exactly. The reason is obvious. First, we have to know *what* they want to kill before we know if it's okay to kill it. If it's a spider, smash it. If it's their little brother, time for a talk. Does that make sense to you?"
>
> "Sure, so far."
>
> "So, let's apply that reasoning to the abortion question using our basic question, 'What is it?' Here's my thinking. If the unborn *is not* a human being, then no justification for abortion is *necessary*.[3] Do what you want. Have the abortion. Do you agree with that?"

---

2. Some might say the next question is "Why? Why do you want to kill this?" If they do, remind them their back is turned, then ask, "Isn't there a more important question to ask *first*?"

3. I suggest that you memorize this statement.

"Of course I do. I'm pro-choice."

"Good. Next step. However, if the unborn *is* a human being, then no justification for abortion is *adequate*."[4]

"Well, I'm not sure about that one."

"Fair enough. Let me clarify with another question. Though the answer may seem obvious, play along for a moment. Here it is: Do you think it's okay to kill a defenseless human being for the reasons most people give for abortion: a right to privacy or choice, the human is too expensive, they interfere with a career, and so on?"

"Of course not. But a fetus isn't a human."

"We'll get to that in a minute. So, in principle you agree with those two general statements—if the unborn is *not* a human being, get the abortion; if it *is* a human, killing it wouldn't be right?"

"Well, I guess—so far."

> **Ambassador Skills**
>
> Some pro-lifers hold there are a number of questions in play, but I'm convinced that this single issue is foundational to addressing all other variations and potential pushbacks—even those affirming the full humanity and full personhood of the unborn.

3. Here's the key line of thinking I'm seeking to establish so far:
    a. Abortion involves killing and discarding something that's alive.
    b. Whether it's right or wrong to kill any living thing depends on what that thing is.
    c. We do not kill defenseless human beings for the reasons most people give to justify abortion.
4. There's nothing complicated or tricky here.

---

4. Memorize this one, too.

a. All we need to do is answer one simple question: What is the unborn?
b. Yet this is the one question that's almost completely ignored.
c. All the popular wordplay now is about the mother: the mother's choice, the mother's career, the mother's financial circumstances, the mother's time, the mother's convenience, the mother's rights—relativism, full tilt.

5. Since these conversations often encounter resistance, I've included this next one for two reasons.
   a. First, it's an example of how to navigate resistance.
   b. Second, it reinforces the "Only One Question" approach.

"Abortion is a private choice between a woman and her doctor."

"Do you mind if I ask you a question? Do we allow parents to abuse their children in privacy with the consent of their doctor?"

"Of course not, but that's not fair. Those children are real people."

"I agree. But it shows that the issue isn't really privacy at all, but rather whether or not the unborn is a human being, right?"

"But lots of poor women can't afford to raise another child."

"I understand. But when kids get too expensive, can we kill them?"

"Of course not, but aborting a fetus is not the same as killing a kid."

"So once again, the real question is 'What is the unborn?' Is a fetus a human just like a youngster?"

"Why do you insist on being so simplistic? Killing defenseless human beings is one thing. Aborting a fetus is another."

"But if abortion actually killed a defenseless human being, wouldn't that be different?"

"Listen, do you really think a woman should be forced to bring an unwanted child into the world?"

"Well, many homeless people are unwanted. Can we kill them?"

"It's not the same!"

"That's the issue, then, isn't it? Are they the same? If the unborn are truly human like the homeless, then we can't just kill them to get them out of the way. We're back to my first question, 'What is the unborn?'"

"But you still shouldn't force your morality on women."

"I get your point, but would you 'force your morality' on a mother who was physically abusing her two-year-old?"

"Sure, but that's not the same."

"Why not?"

"Because you're assuming the unborn is human, like a two-year-old."

"And you're assuming she's not. I get it. We have a genuine difference of opinion here. But what our conversation shows is that the abortion question is not ultimately about privacy or economic hardship or not being wanted or forcing morality. The real question is 'What is the unborn?'"

> **Ambassador Skills**
>
> You might think of other concerns I haven't mentioned. Each can be dispatched with a simple test question, though. Ask, "Would your point work if we were talking about a clear-case example of a human being, like a two-year-old?" This tactic has a name: "Trotting Out the Toddler." For any reason a person gives to justify abortion, ask if the same reason would justify killing a toddler.

6. Notice, at this stage I'm not arguing that the unborn is a human being, or even that abortion is wrong. I'm simply clarifying—and simplifying—the issue.

III. Moral Logic

A. Next, I want to give you the simple moral logic of the pro-life position.[5] Here it is:

Premise 1: It's wrong to intentionally take the life of an innocent human being.

---

5. I use the phrase "moral logic" because this is a logically valid syllogism with moral terms in both a premise and the conclusion.

Premise 2: Abortion intentionally takes the life of an innocent human being. Therefore, abortion is wrong.

🗨 Reflect a Moment

Notice a couple of things immediately. First, the *form* of the argument is right. The conclusion follows naturally from the first two statements. That's easy to see. This, then, is what logicians call a *valid* argument. So far, so good. If the premises turn out to be true, then it is also a *sound* argument—that is, completely reliable based on the simple force of logic. But are the premises true? That's the next step.

1. The first statement seems obviously correct.
2. The pushback is going to be on the second—that the unborn is a human being and not simply a blob of the mother's tissue.
3. Your goal now is to show that the unborn is a human being because . . .
   a. It's growing, so it's *alive*.
   b. It's a *separate being* inside the mother, yet is completely distinct from the mother's body.
   c. And the kind of being growing in her body is a *human being*.
4. Now I want to offer a rather long interaction, but I think you'll see how the conversation addresses each of those issues.

> "The government shouldn't tell me what I can do with my own body."
>
> "I think that's generally true, but can the government say what you can do with your body concerning your two-year-old?" ["Trotting Out the Toddler"]
>
> "That's different. He's outside my body. We're talking about my uterus. They can't dictate what I can do with my uterus any more than they can force me to donate my kidney."
>
> "I agree with you about your kidney, but what does that have to do with the pro-life view? [Columbo #1] Do you think pro-lifers are asking you to give up your uterus?"
>
> "No, but they want to tell me what I can do with my uterus."

"It seems to me there's a misunderstanding here. Pro-lifers are saying the government should be able to protect a separate human being growing *inside* your body just like it does a separate human being growing *outside* your body."

"But we're talking about my uterus, not a human being like an infant."

"I thought we were talking about what was *in* your uterus."

"Okay, but that's not a human being."

"Really? Then what is it?" [Columbo #1]

"It's a blob of tissue."

"Sure, but aren't we all blobs of tissue?"

"That's different."

"How, exactly?" [Columbo #1]

"We're living people, not just tissue."

"Do you mind if I ask you a few questions about this blob inside the uterus of a pregnant woman?"

"Go ahead."

"Is this thing alive?"

"No one really knows when life begins."

"That wasn't quite the question. I asked if it was alive, not when life begins. So let me ask another way. Is this blob inside a pregnant woman's uterus growing?"

"Yes, it's growing."

"How can it be growing if it's not alive?"

"Hmm . . . Okay, you've made your point. It's alive. It's living tissue, part of my own body, and the government has no say over my tissue growing in my body."

"I'm sympathetic with that point in principle, but I don't think this tissue in your body is actually *part* of your body, strictly speaking."

"Of course it is."

"When on a detective show the forensic pathologist finds remains of a human body, how do they know which person the remains belong to?"

"They do a matching DNA test."

"Right. If the DNA from the tissue matches the DNA sample from a known individual, then they know the remains they discovered were part of that person's body."

"Right."

"So, if you were pregnant, and someone took a DNA test of the piece of tissue growing in your uterus—that blob—would its DNA match your DNA?"

"Well . . . no."

"Right. Then whatever is growing inside your body when you're pregnant is not your body, is it? It has different DNA, so it must be a different body. Does that make sense to you?"

"I guess so."

"So, here's the next question: What kind of foreign tissue would be growing inside your uterus if you were pregnant?"

"I can't say for sure."

"Well, let's go back to detective shows again. If forensic pathologists found a piece of tissue at a crime scene, how would they know if that tissue came from a human being or from some other creature?"

"I guess they'd do another DNA test."

"Right, but this test isn't looking to identify a certain *individual*, but rather a certain *kind* of individual—maybe human, maybe some other organism, right?"

"Okay."

"So, if we took a piece of tissue from that living thing growing in your uterus that's not you but something else, what kind of DNA do you think it would have?"

"I don't know. I'm not a scientist."

"I don't think you need to be a scientist to know the answer to this question. Let me ask it another way. What kinds of things naturally and predictably grow inside a pregnant woman's uterus?"

"Well, offspring."

"Good. So we agree on that. Now, if there's an 'offspring' growing in a woman's uterus, what *kind* of offspring do you think it is?"

"I guess it would be a human offspring. But that doesn't mean it's a human being. After all, the unborn doesn't look like a human being."

"Sure she does. She looks exactly the way all human beings look at that stage of development. Look at your own baby pictures, then look at your high school pictures, then look at you now. Do you look the same?"

"Of course not."

"Right. Do you see the point? Living things never look the same at one stage of development as they do at another."

"But that's different."

"Okay, let me put it another way. If you had a cat that was pregnant, what kind of fetus would it be carrying?"

"A cat fetus, I guess."

"Right."

"But an acorn's not an oak. It's a seed."

"Agreed. What kind of seed?"

"An oak seed."

"Right. An acorn is an oak in the seed stage, and a full-grown tree is an oak in a mature stage. But they're both oaks, right?"

"But the unborn is just a zygote or a fetus or whatever."

"Right, but what *kind* of zygote or fetus or whatever?"

"Human?"

"Exactly. Do living things change from one kind of being into another over time, or do they stay themselves?"

"Well, I guess they stay the same thing from beginning to end."

"Right. So, it looks like we know a lot about what's growing inside a pregnant woman's uterus, don't we? It's not merely her tissue, but her human offspring. Someone else—an unborn human being—is in there at varying stages of development. So now that we've solved that mystery, let me take this a step farther. Do you think the government should be allowed to protect your offspring when the child is outside your body but not when he's inside your body?"

"Yes, I do."

"Tell me, why should the government be allowed to protect your offspring on the *outside* of your body—child abuse and stuff like that?"

"Because children are valuable."

"Right, I agree. But that creates a problem for you now, doesn't it?"

"How?"

"Well, if your children are valuable outside your body—say, right after they're born—why aren't those same children valuable just a couple of inches away, hidden inside your body? Why does the mere location of your child make any difference to the value of your child?"

5. So, it's clear that our second premise is solid: the unborn is a human being whose life is taken during abortion.

> **Ambassador Skills**
>
> You see how this works. Of course, those who have strong pro-choice convictions are not likely to change their minds immediately, but your tactical questions have forced them to think about the facts that matter instead of parrying with rhetoric that simply obscures the real issue.

IV. The "Personhood" Shell Game[6]

A. At this point, you may encounter another dodge.
1. Maybe the unborn is a human but not a person.
2. This move takes exception with the first premise.
    a. It's not true that it's wrong to take the life of innocent human *beings*.
    b. It's only wrong to take the life of innocent human *persons*.

---

6. A shell game is a trick used as a quick con to cheat someone using three nutshells or cups that are shuffled to disguise the location of an object under one of them.

B. **When you hear this claim, you must—without exception—ask this question: "What's the difference?"**[7]

 1. What's the difference between a disposable human being and a valuable human person?[8]
 2. It's essential that the person has an answer to this question. Here's why.
    a. They've divided humans into two distinct categories—human persons and human nonpersons.
       (1) Those in the first group have the full protection of law.
       (2) Those in the second group can be killed for virtually any reason.
    b. So you must be absolutely clear who is on one side of that line and who is on the other.

C. **Sometimes the pro-choice person will offer a list of attributes necessary for a mere human to qualify as a valuable person.**

 1. These lists vary, of course. Different people have different criteria.
 2. If they give a list, ask more questions:
    a. Where did you get the list?
    b. What makes one person's list better than another person's list?
    c. Who decides which humans qualify for protection and which don't?
    d. What about lists that exclude black people or Jews or Muslim Serbs or the mentally defective or members of the LGBT community?
    e. These are all examples, by the way, of "human nonpersons" of the past.

D. **You see my point.**

 1. The personhood disqualifier has a dark history.
 2. It's nothing more than crafty legal language meant to disqualify some bona fide members of the human family from being protected members of the human community.

---

7. Notice how frequently I fall back on the first step of our game plan—gathering information—using various forms of our first Columbo question, "What do you mean by that?"

8. Be prepared for a blank stare when you ask this question. The distinction they've just made is almost never based on principle—most have never really thought about it. Often it's just a rhetorical dodge to dismiss your view.

> **Reflect a Moment**
>
> This ruse has been tried before, and history is strewn with the wreckage—from the Dred Scott decision of 1857, declaring black slaves chattel property, to the "Final Solution," when the Third Reich decreed that millions of humans had no inherent right to live and were eliminated as *lebensunwertes Leben*—"life unworthy of life."

E. **No matter what list of qualities someone offers you, items on that list are either going to be completely arbitrary or will disqualify clear-case examples of valuable people. For example:**
   1. Size or physical appearance—the unborn doesn't *look* like a person.
   2. Level of development—the unborn *lacks abilities* real persons have.
   3. Environment—the unborn isn't *located* in the same place as real persons (inside the womb, not outside).
   4. Degree of dependency—the unborn is too *physically dependent* on others to be a person.[9]

It turns out there is no meaningful moral difference between a human being and a human person. None.

F. **Note our basic strategy:**
   1. One, the unborn is alive.
   2. Two, the unborn is not Mom's body, but a separate, individual being.
   3. Three, the unborn is a human being.
   4. Four, there's no meaningful difference between a human being and a human person.

G. **So, the moral logic of the pro-life position stands.**
   1. The unborn is a living being, separate from her mother.
   2. The kind of being she happens to be is human.
   3. Humans are valuable in themselves . . .
      a. Not for what they look like

---

9. This list of distinctions, commonly known as the "SLED test," was first introduced by Stephen Schwarz in *The Moral Question of Abortion* (Chicago: Loyola University Press, 1990).

b. Not for what they can do

c. Not for where they're located

d. Not for their lack of dependency on others

4. Therefore, abortion is terribly wrong.

H. **Here is one other question you might ask your friend: "Were you ever an unborn child?"**

1. Does it make sense to talk about the way you were before you were born?

2. If *you* were the unborn child your mother carried, then abortion would have killed *you*.

   a. Not a potential you

   b. Not a possible you

   c. Not a future you

3. Abortion would have killed *you*.

I. **So, that's our basic case against abortion.**

1. Nowadays, though, you'll often need to take the issue further.

2. Next I offer dialogues modeling responses to various rejoinders you'll likely encounter.

3. I'll conclude with a powerful scriptural approach to answer anyone who says they're a Bible-believing Christian yet still defends abortion.

V. "My Body, My Choice"

A. **The first challenge is one we've already touched on.**

1. It's called "my body, my choice."

2. Also called the "personal autonomy" or "sovereign zone" argument, a woman has the right to do whatever she wants with her own body.

B. **Here are the problems:**

1. First, the basis for the claim is simply not true.

Abortion: Only One Question ▪ 189

   a. People in a civilized society do not have the unrestricted right to do whatever they want with their own bodies.
   b. The law routinely straps all kinds of restrictions on our bodies. It's called *civilization*.
2. Second—and we covered this earlier—the unborn is not the mother's body.
3. Third, no one has the right to kill another human being just because he interferes with the person's life.
4. Here's how I might work those insights into a sample conversation:[10]

> "It's my body, so abortion is my choice."
>
> "Well, I believe in individual liberty, but I think you may be missing something. Can you clarify what you mean?" [Columbo #1]
>
> "Sure. It's simple. I get to do what I want with my body. It belongs to me, not you and not the government. Getting an abortion, then, is my choice and no one else's."
>
> "Got it. But do you really think that principle always applies? I mean, there are lots of laws telling both of us what to do with our bodies: traffic laws, trespassing laws, airport laws—stuff like that. You're not against those, are you?" [Columbo #1]
>
> "Of course not. But abortion is different."
>
> "Do you mind if I ask you another question?"
>
> "Go ahead."
>
> "If you had a two-year-old daughter and wanted to take a vacation, could you leave her home alone while you went to Tahiti—since you can do whatever you want with your own body?"
>
> "Don't be ridiculous. That's different."
>
> "How?"
>
> "Because that's my baby, and she's dependent on me."

---

10. Be careful not to be robotic with these scripts. There's no need to follow the exchanges exactly as they appear here. Instead, use the sample questions to set your course and inform your strategy. Each conversation has its own life, and sometimes—especially with emotional issues like abortion—you'll need to stretch things out to soften the tone.

"Right. So it sounds like you're saying some obligations toward your child properly restrict what you do with your body. So, it's not entirely accurate that you have a right to do *whatever* you want with your own body. Is that fair?"

"Yes, but like I said, abortion is different."

"I get your point, but just so I'm clear, it now looks like you don't think a woman can do *whatever* she wants with her own body, do you?"

"No, I guess not."

"So sometimes restrictions on a person's freedom are okay, right?"

"I see your point."

C. My goal here is simple.

1. I want the pro-choice person to admit it's completely acceptable to limit individual freedom in certain situations.

2. That's all. Nothing complicated. It's not even controversial once the point is clarified.

VI. Right to Refuse

A. Another form of the "my body, my choice" challenge is called the "right to refuse" argument.[11]

1. No woman should be forced to use her body as a life-support system for someone else.[12]

2. She has the "right to refuse," even if refusing to help would result in the other person losing his life.

3. Lots of analogies are offered to make this point—including Judith Jarvis Thomson's famous "violinist" argument.[13]

---

11. Both the "sovereign zone" and the "right to refuse" terminology were coined by Trent Horn.

12. Of course, no one "connected" the mother to her fetus in an artificial way for life support. The woman is making the baby herself, a natural result of behavior she consented to, in most cases.

13. Judith Jarvis Thomson, "A Defense of Abortion," *Philosophy and Public Affairs* 1, no. 1 (Fall 1971): 48–49, https://

4. The basic problem with all of them is that they imply that when a mother doesn't volunteer to be pregnant, she has no more responsibility for her *own* child than she has for a *stranger*.[14]

B. **Here's the most powerful point you want to make with the "right to refuse" argument:**
   1. There's a difference between refusing to help save another's life and actively killing that person.
   2. With abortion, a mother doesn't just withhold aid; she kills her baby.
   3. A conversation on this challenge might look like this:

   "No one should be forced to donate a kidney to help someone else if she doesn't want to."

   "So, if you encountered a sick patient who needed your kidney to survive, you could help if you wanted to, but you shouldn't be forced to help, right?" [Columbo #1]

   "Right."

   "Got it. So, if you were faced with a circumstance like that, what would your options be?"

   "I could choose to help the person if I wanted, or not help, obviously. It's my choice."

   "But there's another option isn't there?"

   "What's that?"

   "You could kill him. That would remove the problem, wouldn't it?"

   "That's ridiculous!"

   "Of course it is. But isn't that the option you face with abortion?"

   "What do you mean?"

---

eclass.uoa.gr/modules/document/file.php/PPP475/Thomson%20Judith%20Jarvis%2C%20A%20defense%20of%20abortion.pdf.

14. One variation claims the unborn child is actually attacking the mother, and therefore abortion is a legitimate act of self-defense. See Eileen McDonagh, *Breaking the Abortion Deadlock: From Choice to Consent* (New York: Oxford University Press, 1996). I deal with both Thomson's violinist argument and McDonagh's self-defense argument in "Unstringing the Violinist," Stand to Reason, February 4, 2013, www.str.org/w/unstringing-the-violinist.

"Well, you could choose to help the baby in your womb by carrying it to term like you might help the person who needs your kidney."

"Right."

"But if you're pregnant, you can't simply choose not to help, can you?"

"Why not?"

"Because you can't just walk away from a pregnancy. That's not one of your options. What do you do instead?"

"I have an abortion."

"Right, and what does abortion do?"

"Well, it kills the fetus."

"Exactly. If you choose abortion, then you're choosing to kill the baby. So, your options are either to carry or to kill. That's all. No walking away. No merely 'refusing to help.' Can you think of any other option?"

"Not at the moment."

"So, on your view a woman has a right to refuse to help if she wants. I get that. But why should she have the right to kill someone she doesn't want to help?"

VII. The Equal Rights Argument

A. Here's another alternative in conversations on abortion that's been effective on the street.
  1. It's called the "equal rights argument."[15]
  2. If all people possess basic rights, then all humans must have some quality that entitles them to those rights.

B. Since our pro-choice friends believe in human rights and human equality, here's the question for them: "What is that quality?"

---

15. This approach is promoted by Steve Wagner of Justice for All (jfaweb.org) and Josh Brahm of the Equal Rights Institute. In fact, much of the material in this section has been informed by Josh Brahm's excellent insights found at equalrightsinstitute.com.

1. What is the one thing we share equally that gives us equal rights?
    a. It turns out, the only thing we all have that other creatures lack is our shared humanity.
    b. But if all humans have those rights, then unborn humans do, too.
    c. Pro-lifers, then, are the ones who consistently promote universal human rights.
2. Here's a sample conversation:

> "In general, are you committed to human rights and human equality?"

"Of course."

> "So, you think we all have an equal right to be protected from violence, etc., right?"

"Absolutely."

> "Gay people, too?"

"Are you kidding?"

> "No, I'm just trying to be clear on a principle we both agree on. So, gay people. Black people? Handicapped people? Trans people? Unwanted homeless people?"

"Yes, of course."

> "I completely agree. Now this next one may seem a little silly, but stay with me. What about possums?"

"You mean the animal? Well, I don't think people should go around killing possums just for fun."

> "Neither do I, but I'm asking if they have the same right to life as other humans."

"Of course not."

> "Why? What do all of us have in common that's different from a possum?"

"We're all humans, and all humans should have equal human rights."

> "So, all those groups I mentioned are members of what you might call the 'equal rights community.'"

"Sure."

"Okay. What about the same kinds of human beings—black or white, gay or straight, handicapped or healthy, wanted or unwanted—before they're born?"

"That's completely different. That's why I'm pro-choice."

"Hmmm. Maybe we can go back to that question of equal rights. You must think there's something we all share equally that makes us equal. What do you think that is?"

"Well, maybe it's because those who are already born are self-aware."

"So are possums."

"I mean humans who are self-aware, not animals."

"A newborn is human, but not self-aware, yet I know you're not saying infants don't have a right to be protected."

"Of course not."

"So, self-awareness can't be the thing that gives us equal rights. We're back to the same question, then: What do all of us share that gives us equal rights, even though we're so different?"

"I can't explain it."

"Would you like to hear what I think all humans share that gives them an equal right to life?"

"Sure, why not."

"How about this: our human nature. It's the only thing we share equally. Therefore, our shared humanity is the valuable thing that gives us human rights. That's why they call them 'human rights,' after all. Does that make sense to you?"

"I never thought of that."

"It's why racism and sexism are wrong, because they deprive people of rights based on differences that don't matter to their value."

"I agree."

"Good. But isn't human nature the same thing unborn humans have, too?"

3. Here's one more short conversation that might help you parry another common dismissal.

"You're a guy. You don't have a uterus."

"True enough, but I'm not clear what difference that makes."

"Since men don't get pregnant, what a woman does with her body is none of their business."

"That confuses me. In a sentence, why do you think I object to abortion?"

"Well, you say it kills a baby."

"Right. So, if abortion actually does kill a baby, then why would it matter if a man or a woman objected?"

"I don't get it."

"Would you object if I was abusing my wife?"

"Of course!"

"But you're not married to her. I am."

"That's irrelevant. If you're hurting someone else, that's wrong. It doesn't matter who objects."

"My point exactly."

Sometimes you'll be talking with a person who is pro-choice but also identifies as a Christian. I don't usually bring the Bible up with abortion, but in this case, I think it's a good idea.

VIII. The Bible and Abortion

A. Scripture doesn't address abortion directly.

1. Rather, abortion falls under a broader biblical principle, the sixth commandment: "You shall not murder" (Ex. 20:13).
2. Why? Here's God's reason.
    a. Back in Genesis, God said, "Whoever sheds man's blood, by man his blood shall be shed, *for in the image of God He made man*" (Gen. 9:6, emphasis added).
    b. Because humans bear God's image, if one human destroys another human, he sacrifices his own life.

B. **So, here is our biblical question regarding abortion:**
   1. Are unborn humans image bearers *in the same sense* God was referring to in Genesis 9:6?
   2. In God's eyes, are humans *before* they're born the very same valuable individuals they are *after* they're born?

C. **Let's see . . .**
   1. Luke 1 records a remarkable exchange between Mary and her cousin Elizabeth—John the Baptist's mother—soon after Jesus is conceived in Mary by the Holy Spirit.

   > When Elizabeth heard Mary's greeting, the baby leaped in her womb; and Elizabeth was filled with the Holy Spirit. And she cried out with a loud voice and said, "Blessed are you among women, and blessed is the fruit of your womb! And how has it happened to me, that the mother of my Lord would come to me? For behold, when the sound of your greeting reached my ears, the baby leaped in my womb for joy." (Luke 1:41–44)

   2. This took place when . . .
      a. Elizabeth was in her late second trimester with John.
      b. Mary was in her early first trimester with Jesus.
      c. Clearly, John, the "fetus," was filled with the Holy Spirit and leapt with joy in the presence of the "embryo," Jesus, the Lord.
   3. So, here's our question again:
      a. According to Scripture, were John the Baptist and Jesus their same selves *before* they were born as they were *after* they were born?
      b. Clearly, the biblical answer is yes. Had Mary and Elizabeth chosen abortion, then they would have killed Jesus and John themselves.

D. **Abortion, then—in *God's* eyes—is murder.**
   1. No Christian should condone it.

2. No Christian should participate in it.
   3. Every Christian should condemn it.[16]

🗨 Reflect a Moment

Having a baby under any circumstance is a challenge, but especially so when the pregnancy is unplanned or the result of a traumatic experience. Even so, these complications do not change the basic biblical calculus. Abortion violates the sixth commandment.

E. **By the way, is murder a forgivable sin?**
   1. Of course it is. Even the apostle Paul was a murderer.
   2. No sin is so great that the grace of God can't cover it.

F. **As you've probably noticed, these conversations often overlap in content.**
   1. That's because we're using the same strategy in each case—the moral logic of the pro-life position based on the central question, "What is the unborn?"
   2. Most pro-choice arguments can be addressed by using questions to apply those concepts to any pro-choice challenge.

IX. What Main Points Did We Cover in This Session?

A. **First, we focused on the one question that needs to be answered to answer the question of the morality of abortion: What is the unborn?**
   1. If the unborn *is not* a human being, then no justification for abortion is necessary.
   2. If the unborn *is* a human being, then no justification for abortion is adequate.

---

16. I'm dealing only with the ethical status of abortion here, not the more complex policy concern of how we prosecute abortion within our legal system. That is a different question I'll leave to others more skilled in those matters. With legal judgments, facts always come first, then legislation appropriate to the facts. In the case of abortion, Scripture makes the moral facts clear.

B. **Second, we covered the moral logic of the pro-life view.**
   1. Premise 1: It's wrong to intentionally take the life of an innocent human being.
   2. Premise 2: Abortion intentionally takes the life of an innocent human being.
   3. Therefore, abortion is wrong.

C. **Third, we showed that the unborn is a living human being, separate from the mother's body.**
   1. The unborn has a different DNA "fingerprint" than the mother.
   2. The unborn's DNA "signature" is human.

D. **Fourth, we dealt with a few common objections.**
   1. The "human but not a person" objection
      a. The most important response to this claim is "What's the difference?"
      b. When a person gives a list of criteria distinguishing nonvaluable human beings from valuable human persons, ask:
         (1) Where did you get the list?
         (2) What makes one person's list better than another person's list?
         (3) Who decides which humans qualify for protection and which don't?
      c. Any list is going to be arbitrary and/or will disqualify clear-case examples of valuable people (the SLED test).
   2. The "my body, my choice" challenge
      a. People in a civilized society do not have the unrestricted right to do whatever they want with their own bodies.
      b. The unborn is not the mother's body but is a separate human being her body is producing as her natural offspring.
   3. The "right to refuse" challenge
      a. Claim: we may have a right to refuse helping a person whose life depends on our assistance or care.
      b. But we do not have the right to kill that person to avoid that burden.

E. **We then saw how only the pro-life view consistently supports universal human rights.**

1. All humans have something that unifies their common right to life.
2. The only thing we all share in common is our human nature.
3. Since the unborn shares that human nature, only the pro-life view consistently supports equal human rights for *all* humans.

F. Finally, we learned from Scripture that in God's eyes abortion violates the sixth commandment against murder.
1. It's clear from the Gospel of Luke that both Jesus and John the Baptist were "themselves" while still in their mothers' wombs.
2. If their mothers would have had abortions, then they would have killed Jesus and John.

❓ Self-Assessment

Try to answer the following questions without using your notes.

1. What does Greg call the approach that focuses on the linchpin issue regarding the morality of abortion?
    ➤ The approach is called "_____ One _____."

2. What is the single question that needs to be answered to determine the moral legitimacy of abortion?
    ➤ That question is "What is the _____?"

3. What is the question that's tied to an analogy to make this point?
    ➤ The question is "Mommy/Daddy, can I _____ this?"

4. What are the two contrasting statements that clarify the basic moral calculus regarding abortion?
    ➤ If the unborn is not a _____ being, then no justification for abortion is _____. However, if the unborn is a human _____, then no justification for abortion is _____.

5. Describe the "Trotting Out the Toddler" tactic.
    ▸ Whenever a _____ is given for abortion, ask if the same justification would apply to taking the life of a _____.

6. List the three steps of the moral logic of the pro-life position.
    ▸ Premise 1: It's wrong to _____ take the life of an _____ human being.
    ▸ Premise 2: Abortion _____ takes the life of an innocent _____ being.
    ▸ Therefore, abortion is _____.

7. List the three things we argue for to support premise 2.
    ▸ One, the unborn is _____. Two, the unborn is not the mother's _____ but is a _____ individual _____. Three, the unborn is a _____ being.

8. What's the most important question to ask when someone says the unborn is a human but not a person?
    ▸ The most important question is "What's the _____?"

9. What does the acronym SLED stand for in the "SLED test"?
    ▸ S_____, L_____ of development, E_____, Degree of _____

10. What are three basic errors with the "my body, my choice" argument?
    ▸ First, no one has the _____ to do whatever they want with their own _____. Second, the unborn is not the mother's _____. Third, no one has the right to _____ another human being just because he _____ with their life.

11. What is the "right to refuse" argument?
    ▸ No woman should be forced to use her _____ as a life-_____ system for someone else.

12. What is the most powerful point to use to rebut the "right to refuse" argument?
    ▸ There's a difference between _____ to help save another's life and actively _____ that person.

13. What is the basic question we can use to make the equal rights argument?
    ➤ What is the one thing we _____ equally that gives us all equal _____?

14. What is the answer to that question?
    ➤ The one thing we share equally that gives us all _____ rights is our shared human _____.

15. How does that observation inform the abortion debate?
    ➤ If all humans have those rights by virtue of being _____, then unborn humans have _____ human _____, too.

16. What command in the Bible implicitly condemns abortion?
    ➤ The _____ commandment: "You shall not _____."

17. What is the best chapter in Scripture to use to demonstrate that in God's eyes a human being is the same individual before he's born as after he's born?
    ➤ The best chapter is _____.

18. What does that passage show?
    ➤ The passage shows that John the Baptist was _____ with the _____ when he was still a _____ because he was in the presence of the Lord Jesus when he was an _____.

☑ Self-Assessment with Answers

1. The approach is called "**Only** One **Question**."
2. That question is "What is the **unborn**?"
3. The question is "Mommy/Daddy, can I **kill** this?"
4. If the unborn is not a **human** being, then no justification for abortion is **necessary**. However, if the unborn is a human **being**, then no justification for abortion is **adequate**.
5. Whenever a **justification** is given for abortion, ask if the same justification would apply to taking the life of a **toddler**.

6. Premise 1: It's wrong to **intentionally** take the life of an **innocent** human being. Premise 2: Abortion **intentionally** takes the life of an innocent **human** being. Therefore, abortion is **wrong**.
7. One, the unborn is **alive**. Two, the unborn is not the mother's **body** but is a **separate** individual **being**. Three, the unborn is a **human** being.
8. The most important question is "What's the **difference**?"
9. **Size**, **Level** of development, **Environment**, Degree of **dependency**
10. First, no one has the **right** to do whatever they want with their own **body**. Second, the unborn is not the mother's **body**. Third, no one has the right to **kill** another human being just because he **interferes** with their life.
11. No woman should be forced to use her **body** as a life-**support** system for someone else.
12. There's a difference between **refusing** to help save another's life and actively **killing** that person.
13. What is the one thing we **share** equally that gives us all equal **rights**?
14. The one thing we share equally that gives us all **equal** rights is our shared human **nature**.
15. If all humans have those rights by virtue of being **human**, then unborn humans have **equal** human **rights**, too.
16. The **sixth** commandment: "You shall not **murder**."
17. The best chapter is **Luke 1**.
18. The passage shows that John the Baptist was **filled** with the **Holy Spirit** when he was still a **fetus** because he was in the presence of the Lord Jesus when he was an **embryo**.

Interactive Group Study Questions

1. Discuss why the "Only One Question" approach is central to addressing all attempts at justifying abortion.
2. Talk about the basic line of thinking that I've used here to defend the unborn. Why is this step-by-step sequence important?
3. Describe the "Trotting Out the Toddler" tactic. What is the purpose of the tactic, and how do you think it helps clarify the issue?
4. Talk a bit about the moral logic of the pro-life position. Discuss the difference between

a valid argument and a sound argument. How might you couple the moral logic with tactical questions to get a pro-choice person thinking more clearly about abortion?

5. Discuss how you would navigate a conversation with someone who uses the "personhood" maneuver to dismiss the value of the unborn. Talk about some of the qualities they might offer to define personhood. What are the liabilities of using those criteria to determine human value?
6. Explain the "right to refuse" argument. Talk about why it is a compelling argument for some people; then discuss its fatal weakness.
7. Discuss the equal rights argument against abortion. Think together about how a pro-abortion advocate might counter it and what your own response to that person might be.
8. Scripture doesn't address abortion directly. Instead, abortion falls under a broader biblical principle. What is that principle, and why, scripturally, does it properly apply to abortion?

💡 Going Deeper: Information for Self-Study

Explain to a friend the things you've covered in this lesson.
1. Describe for him the "Only One Question" concept.
2. Do your best to explain why no version of the "my body, my choice" argument justifies abortion, and include the human rights angle if you can.
3. Explain the flaw in the "right to refuse" argument.
4. Explain why only the pro-life view secures equal rights for all humans.
5. Finally, on your own, try working out a conversation using questions that employ the biblical rationale against abortion.
6. Be prepared to share your experiences with the group when you get together next time.

🍎 Food for Thought

More Gore

Over the course of two and a half centuries before abolition, at least 388,000 Africans were shipped to North America.[17] Abortion kills that many children in this country—

---

17. "The Middle Passage," National Park Service, last updated December 2, 2021, www.nps.gov/articles/the-middle-passage.htm.

including a disproportionate number of black babies—in 109 days. Abortion in America has killed nearly as many human beings as all the Allied soldiers, all the Axis armies, and all the civilians from both sides put together who perished in World War II.[18]

The "Elephant" Man

Sometimes human bodies look familiar, healthy, and normal; other times they look odd and unusual. In rare cases—and many of us have seen them—the body looks all wrong, yet the valuable human being is still there.

The movie *The Elephant Man* was a remarkable chronicle of the life of Joseph Merrick (called "John" in the film), a human being grotesquely misshapen from birth. He was caged, whipped, and treated like an animal until a compassionate doctor took him under his care.

A scene from that film is etched into my memory. One night Merrick ventures out of the hospital on his own, cloaked and hooded to hide his disfigurement. A child catches a glimpse of his face, however, and screams. Merrick begins to run. Men who'd heard the screams take up the chase. As he runs faster, weaving in and out of the throng, his hood comes off, exposing his horrible face. There are more screams, and more bystanders join the pursuit. No one knows what crime has been committed, only that a hideous creature has been put to flight.

The mob, with walking sticks and fists upraised, corners the Elephant Man, intent on destroying the monster. In a moment of desperation, Merrick faces his tormentors and cries out, "I am not an animal. I . . . am a human being." The crowd goes silent and hovers over him for one perilous moment. Then, as his words sink in, each person turns away in shame, leaving Merrick trembling in the shadows.

Joseph Merrick, the Elephant Man, was a human being just like you and me. So are millions of others who are odd, misshapen, and severely handicapped. So are the unborn. Humans are valuable even if their physical bodies are so distorted or so small that their humanity is unrecognizable to us. Human worth transcends physical appearance—skin color, size, disfigurements, handicaps—because physical form is irrelevant to significance.

---

18. Mack Dean, "World War 2 Casualties," worldwar2facts.org, February 6, 2021, www.worldwar2facts.org/world-war-2-casualties.html.

Therefore, "not looking right" cannot disqualify any human being from value. Otherwise, there's no defense against racism and ethnic cleansing.

Deadly Word Games

Solomon said, "Death and life are in the power of the tongue."[19] Another famous saying goes, "When words lose their meanings, people lose their lives." Language, carefully chosen, can make evil look good and vice seem like virtue—with drastic consequences.

Case in point. Years ago, I read Robert J. Lifton's *The Nazi Doctors: Medical Killing and the Psychology of Genocide*.[20] Lifton's goal was to answer how doctors who were dedicated to saving life could be persuaded to destroy life on a massive scale. The Nazis succeeded by using language.

Lifton described what he called "killing as a therapeutic imperative,"[21] or, simply, killing in the name of healing. When killing is characterized as healing of any kind, Lifton argued—whether individual healing, social well-being, or cultural cleansing—then that civilization is on the threshold of indescribable evil.

Note the language now in play. Abortion *saves a child* from future physical abuse. Abortion *rescues a baby* with Down syndrome (for example) from an unhappy life. Abortion *protects a mother* from postpartum suicidal thoughts or from the painful recollections of rape. I've seen pro-choice memes that characterize killing an unborn child as compassionate. It's an act of mercy, of love, of healing—a proper means to a noble end. Killing by abortion brings healing. In Lifton's words, this is killing as "therapeutic imperative."

I realize it's risky to invoke a horrid period of human history to make a contemporary moral point. The impulse is strong to dismiss any such comparison as extreme. Nevertheless, with abortion the parallel fits.

---

19. Proverbs 18:21.
20. Robert Jay Lifton, *The Nazi Doctors: Medical Killing and the Psychology of Genocide* (New York: Basic Books/HarperCollins, 1986).
21. Ibid., 15.

SESSION 10

MARRIAGE, SEX, GENDER, AND COMMON SENSE

Demonstrating Mastery

Try recalling the answers to the following questions without using your notes. The answers are in the "Self-Assessment with Answers" section of session 9.

1. What is the single question that needs to be answered to determine the moral legitimacy of abortion?
2. What is the most important question to ask when someone says the unborn is a human but not a person?
3. What does the acronym SLED stand for in the "SLED test"?
4. What is the basic question we can use to make the equal rights argument? What is the answer to that question?
5. What is the best chapter in Scripture to use to demonstrate that in God's eyes a human being is the same individual before he's born as after he's born? What does that passage show?

I. Review and Looking Ahead

A. In the preceding session, we covered the following:

1. First, we focused on the one question that needs to be answered to answer the question of the morality of abortion: What is the unborn?
    a. If the unborn *is not* a human being, then no justification for abortion is necessary.
    b. If the unborn *is* a human being, then no justification for abortion is adequate.
2. Second, we covered the moral logic of the pro-life view.
    a. Premise 1: It's wrong to intentionally take the life of an innocent human being.
    b. Premise 2: Abortion intentionally takes the life of an innocent human being.
    c. Therefore, abortion is wrong.
3. Third, we showed that the unborn is a living human being, separate from the mother's body.
    a. The unborn has a different DNA "fingerprint" than the mother.
    b. The unborn's DNA "signature" is human.
4. Fourth, we dealt with a few common objections.
    a. The "human but not a person" objection
    b. The "my body, my choice" challenge
    c. The "right to refuse" challenge
5. We then saw how only the pro-life view consistently supports universal human rights.
    a. All humans have something that unifies their common right to life.
    b. The only thing we all share in common is our human nature.
    c. Since the unborn shares that human nature, only the pro-life view consistently supports equal human rights for *all* humans.
6. Finally, we learned from Scripture that in God's eyes abortion violates the sixth commandment against murder.

B. Here is what we'll cover in this session:
1. First, I'll address what Jesus did and—allegedly—did not say on the controversial issues of marriage, gender, and sex.
2. Second, I'll help you see what God had in mind from the beginning regarding sex and marriage.

3. Third, I'll tell you why pronouns matter and how you can navigate those challenging waters.
4. Finally, I'll address the question of the Bible and sex—especially the issue of homosexuality in light of attempts to reinterpret Scripture in a gay-affirming way.

II. Christian Confusion

A. Lately I've been mystified—and distressed—at how easily many who identify as Christian embrace ideas completely at odds with the Bible—especially when it comes to sex.
   1. I think there are two reasons for this.
      a. First, many Christians are untutored in the basics. They just don't know Scripture well.
      b. Second, many—especially in the younger generation—seem to care more about what their friends think of them than about what Jesus thinks of them.
   2. Regarding the first, an encouragement. Getting clear on the truth is not complicated.
      a. The Scripture speaks clearly on these issues. There is no ambiguity.
      b. Plus, no divine insight is even necessary. Simple common sense is all you need to figure out what has been obvious to most of the world until just recently.
      c. Yes, the world is confused. That does not mean you need to be confused.
   3. Regarding the second, a warning.
      a. It's hard to imagine topics more emotionally charged right now than gender, marriage, and sex.
      b. One ethic completely dominates the street, and it is not God's ethic.
      c. The commitment to the world's perspective on these issues is intense, so be ready for pushback and hostility when you side with God.

B. Let's start with what I call the "Silent Christ" objection.

1. Some make the claim that Jesus never condemned homosexuality—or same-sex marriage, or transgenderism, or abortion. So how can Christians condemn those things if their Savior didn't?[1]

🗨 Reflect a Moment

Notice the tactic in play here. People attempt to bolster their point by enlisting Jesus as their ally. Cleary, they want Christ on their side. But why, especially if they're not Christians? Because Jesus has credibility with just about everybody. If Jesus agrees with our critics—or at least appears to—the better for them.

2. Here's my response:
    a. What if Jesus actually *was* silent?
        (1) What if in his entire ministry he never uttered a single word about, say, abortion or homosexuality or gender?
        (2) What can we conclude about Jesus' view on those issues? Nothing. Nothing at all.
    b. Here's why: you can't conclude anything about what Jesus *approved* of based on what he *did not condemn*.
        (1) As far as we know, Jesus didn't say anything about slavery, capital punishment, spousal abuse, sex trafficking, racism, or child sacrifice.
        (2) Does that mean he approved of those things? Of course not.
3. Here's how I might play this point out tactically in a conversation:

"Jesus never said a thing about homosexuality."

"Maybe you're right. But even if he didn't, so what?" [Columbo #1]

"Well, if Jesus was against homosexuality as much as you Christians are, then he'd have said something about it. But he never did."

"I have a couple of questions about that."

"Go ahead."

---

[1]. It's worth noting, though, that many who hold to "Silent Christ" seem to care little about those things he was *not* silent about when it interferes with their personal projects—but that's another issue.

> "Let's say you're right—Jesus never uttered a single word about homosexuality. Do you think that since Jesus never condemned homosexuality, he was okay with it?"
>
> "You got it."
>
> "Well, that would mean Jesus was okay with slavery, too."
>
> "What?!"
>
> "Well, he never mentioned anything about that, as far as we know, so his silence on slavery must mean approval."
>
> "That's ridiculous!"
>
> "I agree with you there, but that creates a problem for you. Are you still comfortable saying that whatever Jesus didn't condemn, he approved of?"
>
> "I'll have to think about that."
>
> "Okay. One last question: If Jesus *did* condemn homosexuality, would you agree with him?"

4. Here's the point:
    a. It's hard to conclude anything about what Jesus did *not* condemn based on the limited written record of what he *did* condemn. Notice I said difficult, not impossible.
    b. Sometimes we can infer Jesus' view based on a related thing he did weigh in on.

Which brings me to my next point:

C. **When Jesus was asked by the Pharisees about divorce, here's what he said:**

Have you not read that He who created them from the beginning made them male and female, and said, "For this reason a man shall leave his father and mother and be joined to his wife, and the two shall become one flesh"? . . . What therefore God has joined together, let no man separate. (Matt. 19:4–6)

1. Note: Jesus answered a challenge regarding marriage by going back to the very beginning, to the creation order.

2. He went back to God's original plan for human flourishing by quoting from Genesis.

D. I don't want you to miss three crucial takeaways from Jesus' teaching on divorce.
   1. First, Jesus affirmed the commonsense observation that human gender is binary.
      a. Human beings are either male or female. God designed them that way.
      b. That's how we reproduce ("Be fruitful and multiply," Gen. 1:28).

▶ Reflect a Moment

There are rare physical exceptions to human binary sexuality—for example, those who are, because of congenital defect, born intersex—but that is not the way things were supposed to be. All congenital abnormalities are a result of the world being broken. It was not God's good design at the start.

   2. Second, marriage is between a man and a woman, a male and a female. Period.
      a. Not between two males or two females (same-sex marriage).
      b. Not between a mixture of males and females (polygamy or polyamory).
      c. According to Jesus, what God intended from the beginning still stands today.
   3. Third, the only kind of sexuality ("one flesh") that is proper in Jesus' view is sex between a man and a woman who are committed to each other for life in marriage.
      a. Conversely, all forms of sex expressly prohibited in the Bible—adultery, fornication, homosexuality, and bestiality—are each automatically disqualified by Jesus' statement.
      b. Jesus' reasoning rules them all out.[2]

▶ Reflect a Moment

Here's the best way I've found to sum up Jesus' view: God's original plan is *one man with one woman, becoming one flesh for one lifetime.* This simple summary covers all the controversial bases. Pretty straightforward, and it's still God's plan.

---

2. Notice these all involve sex with someone other than a person's opposite-sex spouse.

E. There's a reason God made two physical sexes with their matching genders.
   1. He made men and women physically and emotionally different so they would fit together in a complementary way.
   2. He created men and women to be counterparts for each other.
   3. Indeed, without this, it wouldn't be possible for them to multiply.

F. Not only is Scripture clear on this issue, but no culture—Christian or otherwise—has been confused for thousands of years until now.
   1. Gender is not "fluid" the way some people suggest.
   2. That is not how God made human beings.
   3. Imaginations may be fluid, but not gender.

III. Pronouns

A. I know pronouns seem like inconsequential little things . . .
   1. Him, her, he, she. No big deal. Why don't we just play along with "preferred pronouns"? No hassle.
   2. If pronouns really were "inconsequential little things," then why has so much ink been spilled—and, in some cases, livelihoods lost—for not getting them right?
   3. Because getting particular pronouns right means getting a particular narrative right.

B. Here's what's at stake with those simple little words.
   1. We are besieged by a worldview that is completely foreign to Jesus' view of reality.
   2. According to this view, the "truth" about our sex is not "out there" in God's world.
   3. It's "in here," in the internal world of feelings and personal beliefs. That's relativism.

C. In our culture, we are pressured to reject both God's truth and common sense to affirm a false narrative of reality.
   1. Why? Because (they say) it's the only way to be kind.

2. On the pretext of being kind, the world has made pronouns the skirmish line in what is actually a battle of worldviews.
   a. Here's the crux: Who defines reality, God or each one of us?
   b. This pronoun demand is not about being kind; it's about enforcing a foreign worldview.
3. Paul warned us not to be taken captive by the empty deceptions of men (Col. 2:8). The pronoun ploy is one of those empty deceptions.

Reflect a Moment

Amazingly, the obstetrician's announcement "It's a girl!" is now considered child abuse by some since the doctor is arbitrarily "assigning" gender without the baby's consent.

D. **So, what do we do?**
   1. How do we resist the lie, live the truth, and still be kind?
   2. We take a cue from Christ and distinguish the narrative from the individual.
   3. John said Jesus was "full of grace and truth" (John 1:14).
      a. This detail of Christ's character can help us navigate the gender minefield on the street.
      b. We protect people's feelings (show grace)—within reason . . .
      c. But we reject the narrative (uphold truth).

E. **When it comes to pronouns, you will face three separate circumstances that require three different responses.**
   1. First, in my opinion, we should call people by the names they choose for themselves.
      a. Names are different from pronouns; they're personal preferences by nature.
      b. Refusing to call someone by the name they choose for themselves just comes across as mean-spirited (although with your own children you can insist on a name consistent with their biology).
      c. Pronouns, though, refer to sex. One's sex is not a preference. It's a fixed feature of reality.
   2. Second, if you're required to post your "preferred" pronoun, don't simply report your accurate biological gender.

a. That reinforces the lie that pronouns are mere personal preferences and your preference happens to match your sex.
   b. Instead, post this: "I don't have a preferred pronoun. I have a sex. I'm male [for example]." Don't participate in the lie.
3. Third, if you're asked to use preferred pronouns when speaking of others, then graciously—but firmly—refuse.
   a. Say, "This is not my view, so I'd be dishonest and inauthentic to act like it was."
   b. In most cases, pronouns are third-person references anyway—talking about people not present—so their feelings aren't at stake.
   c. Arm-twisting at this point is political, not ethical.
   d. If you're a teacher, you could use students' last names for third-person references if you like or find some other workaround.
      (1) But don't yield to pressure to use pronouns that reflect a peculiar, controversial, and divisive political view that you do not hold.
      (2) That's living a lie.
4. It's also not loving your neighbor.
   a. For those with gender confusion, the suicide rates skyrocket.
   b. Even in Sweden—a culture completely accepting on these issues—the suicide mortality rate for transgender people is twenty times higher than the general population.
   c. Surgery does not improve those numbers, either.[3]
5. There's a reason surgery is not the answer.
   a. For one, it is biologically impossible to change one's sex. Full stop.
   b. The best one can do is mutilate a perfectly healthy body.
   c. Second, those dealing with genuine gender dysphoria are deeply broken people—even by their own admission (for example, "I'm a woman trapped in a man's body").
   d. The solution isn't surgery. The solution is compassionate psychological help.
      (1) They need our grace and love—not our enablement.
      (2) Would we recommend liposuction to an anorexic?

---

3. Paul McHugh, "Transgender Surgery Isn't the Solution," *Wall Street Journal*, May 13, 2016, www.wsj.com/articles/paul-mchugh-transgender-surgery-isnt-the-solution-1402615120.

F. Graciously hold your ground.
1. Refuse to be bullied into affirming a lie.
2. On this issue, our goal is modest.
    a. We do not demand that others abandon *their* views.
    b. We only ask that we be allowed to keep *our* views.
    c. We may not be able to change culture, but we can always keep the culture from changing us.[4]
3. This issue is problematical, so it's difficult to write a dialogue for since the subject itself defies common sense. Here are some starters, though.

> "What is a woman?"[5]
> "A woman is someone who feels like a woman."
> "But you haven't answered my question. What exactly is a woman that anyone would feel like one?"
> "I can't define it. It's something a person feels. How would you define a woman?"
> "Someone who has the innate potential to be a mother because she has female reproductive organs. What else would a woman be?"
> "Someone who feels like a woman."
> "You mean someone who feels like they have a uterus and a vagina, even if they don't actually have them?"
> "Maybe. It's hard to explain."
> "So, is someone with female sexual organs a woman or not?"
> "That depends. If that person feels like a woman, yes. If that person feels like a man, then he's a man."
> "Okay . . . what is a man?"

4. Here's another approach . . .

> "You should use the pronouns people want you to use."
> "Why?"

---

4. See Rod Dreher, *Live Not by Lies: A Manual for Christian Dissidents* (New York: Sentinel, 2020).
5. I owe this line of questioning to Matt Walsh.

"Because it's kind. It shows respect for them. It makes them feel comfortable."

"Do you think a person should be authentic and true to their own beliefs?"

"Of course. That's my point."

"Do you think I should be authentic and true to my own beliefs, too?"

"Sure."

"Then why not be nice to me by respecting my own deeply held beliefs on this issue?"

"Because you're transphobic."

"Why call me names just because I don't agree with you? Is that being kind or respectful?"

Objective binary sexuality is also key to understanding God's purpose for something else the culture has been confused about . . .

IV. Marriage

A. When questioned on divorce, the first thing Jesus said is that God made human beings male and female.
1. Why did Jesus begin with gender when answering a question about marriage?
2. Because God's purpose for marriage is based on gender—binary gender.
    a. "A man shall leave his father and his mother, and be joined to his wife" (Gen. 2:24).
    b. Men marry women. Women marry men.
    c. Men and women become fathers and mothers. That's God's plan.
3. Since children can only come from men (the fathers) physically joined ("one flesh") with women (the mothers), being a man or a woman is determined by one's physical body.
4. Again, no Bible verses are needed to verify this point. It's common sense.

B. According to Jesus' thinking, then, same-sex marriage—or any other variation—is not only wrong for the same reason divorce is wrong (it corrupts God's good design); it is also a contradiction in terms.

1. The word *marriage* has no meaning when used of same-sex couples.
2. Why? Because heterosexual union is inherent to God's design of human bodies for reproduction.

🔖 Reflect a Moment

Stable families are fundamental to stable civilizations. Long-term, monogamous, heterosexual unions—as a group, as a rule, and by nature—produce the next generation. No other relationship serves that vital function. That's the reason societies regulate, privilege, and protect those unique unions. Ensuring their stability is an act of cultural self-preservation.

C. There is nothing ambiguous about Jesus' view.
1. Yes, the culture is confused, but there is no reason for you to be confused.
2. A *good* answer, though, is not always an *acceptable* answer to a critic.
3. Be forewarned: people in the world are easily deluded and often difficult to convince.
4. Here's a sample conversation, though, that might help:

"I think it's good that the government approves same-sex marriage."

"Let me ask you a question. As a rule, what comes first, marriages or families?"

"Marriages."

"Right. Do you think that's a good idea?"

"Sure."

"Why?"

"Because without marriages, moms and kids can't be properly taken care of."

"Exactly. But did you notice what you just assumed?"

"What?"

"That marriages usually create families with children."

"Right. That's the way it usually works."

"Do you think government should intrude on private relationships and regulate them?"

"Of course not."

"But there's lots of government regulations about marriage and families, right?"[6]

"Of course."

"But you don't object to them. Why?"

"Because of the kids."

"So, it sounds like you're saying the government can legitimately intrude in relationships that characteristically have kids, but not if they don't have kids?"

"Sounds right."

"So, if a certain type of relationship never characteristically produced children, the government should stay out?"

"Yes."

"Then I don't understand why you're in favor of same-sex marriage."

Now I want to focus on something else Jesus said.

V. "One Flesh"

A. According to Jesus, in marriage a man cleaves to—and becomes "one flesh" with—a woman, his wife.

1. Their physical bodies are joined together in a deep, profound sexual union.
    a. The two become one.
    b. That is the good purpose of God.
2. The only kind of sexual behavior honorable to God, then, is intimacy between a man and a woman in the lifelong committed relationship of marriage.

B. Consider homosexuality, for example.

1. I know that every depiction of homosexuality in popular culture is overwhelmingly positive.

---

6. Government only privileges relationships that contribute to government interests. It has no interest in stable relationships in general, only in stabilizing particular *kinds* of relationships—generally, economic relations tied to commerce (for example, corporations) and those in which the protection of children is a factor. Inheritance rights flow naturally to progeny. Tax relief for families eases the financial burden children make on paychecks. Insurance policies reflect the unique relationship between a wage earner and his or her dependents.

2. Those who differ are considered hateful bigots.
3. This is not God's perspective, though.

C. I want you to pay close attention to the details of a point Paul makes about homosexuality in Romans:

God gave them over to degrading passions; for . . . the men abandoned the natural function of the woman and burned in their desire toward one another, men with men committing indecent acts. (Rom. 1:26–27)

1. The word translated "function" here is the Greek word *kreesis*.
   a. Paul is talking here about sexual plumbing, so to speak.
   b. God designed men and women to function sexually together. Their bodies fit together in a precise way to make sexual union possible.
2. Notice how Paul explains the nature of this offense in God's eyes.
   a. He says, "The men abandoned the natural *function of the woman*."
   b. They rejected the appropriate counterpart God had provided—a woman who was built by God to be man's sexual complement.
   c. That's why Scripture has nothing positive to say about homosexuality. Whenever it's mentioned in the Bible, it's condemned.

🗨 Reflect a Moment

Since the birth of the church, no Christian authority—no church council, no denominational confession—ever hinted that homosexual behavior was morally legitimate. Now congregations everywhere are becoming "gay affirming," convinced that for two thousand years we've misunderstood the Bible.

Here's what we've missed, according to gay-affirming Christians:

D. Claim: "The same-sex behavior condemned in the Bible is not what modern-day LGBT Christians practice."

1. This is the "not that kind of homosexuality" argument.[7]

---

7. It's also known as the "cultural distance argument."

2. Ancient same-sex behavior was exploitive, abusive, and oppressive—the argument goes—completely unlike the caring, committed, covenantal unions promoted by gay Christians today. Therefore . . .
   a. Scripture doesn't prohibit loyal, loving, same-sex relationships.
   b. It only prohibits abusive forms like pederasty, master-slave exploitation, promiscuity, rape, and so on.
3. Simply put, the church has been interpreting the Bible wrong because it didn't understand ancient culture like we do now.[8]

E. **This attempt fails for a simple reason, and no insight into ancient Near East sexual practices is necessary to see it.**
   1. When it comes to sex, Scripture condemns the *behavior*, not the *relationship*.
      a. Take Leviticus 18:22, for example: "You shall not lie with a male as one lies with a female; it is an abomination."
      b. There's not the slightest hint in Leviticus that same-sex activity is only a problem when it's coercive or oppressive.
      c. Note that under the Law, *both* participants were punished for this offense.
   2. In every passage forbidding homosexuality, the prohibition is unqualified.[9]
      a. There are no exceptions for loving, consensual, committed relationships. None. Again . . .
         (1) The Bible is not condemning perverse *relationships* here.
         (2) It is condemning perverse *behavior*.
      b. The pattern is exactly the same with all sinful sexual activity. Is adultery okay if it is loving and consensual? Is fornication?
   3. Whenever a man lies with a man the way he should be lying with a woman, he's rejecting—once again—the woman who was "fit" for him by God, exchanging her for the man who was not fit for him by God.

---

8. For a detailed treatment of attempts by some within the church to biblically sanitize homosexuality, see Alan Shlemon, "A Reformation the Church Doesn't Need," Stand to Reason, June 30, 2015, www.str.org/w/a-reformation-the-church-doesn-t-need-part-1.

9. For an excellent concise treatment of this issue, see Kevin DeYoung, *What Does the Bible Really Teach about Homosexuality?* (Wheaton, IL: Crossway, 2015).

🔖 Reflect a Moment

Christians don't condone adultery as far as I know, but fornication hardly raises an eyebrow nowadays—especially among the younger crowd. Yet it's just as much a violation of God's good plan as homosexuality.

F. Here is Paul's sobering summary on the status of those who engage in persistent sexual sin:

Do you not know that the unrighteous will not inherit the kingdom of God? Do not be deceived; neither fornicators . . . nor adulterers . . . nor homosexuals . . . will inherit the kingdom of God. (1 Cor. 6:9–10)[10]

1. God's solution for satisfying our sexual appetites is lifelong heterosexual marriage. Confusion on this issue, as Paul points out, is deadly deception. Do not be taken in.
2. God's plan for sex and marriage is built into the structure of the world he made.
    a. Since the beginning of time, this has been obvious to everyone, even those without Bibles.
    b. Times change, but reality does not. God's Word does not change, either.
3. Following is a sampling of dialogues that might help you. Remember this, though:
    a. I never make homosexuality an issue when I do evangelism.
    b. Why not? Because homosexuality—or any other sexual sin—is not the issue. Sin is the issue.
        (1) Straight people need Jesus, too.
        (2) Rebellion against God, not any particular sin, is the real problem.
4. Here's the first conversation:

"Does God hate gays?"
   "Why would you think that?" [Columbo #1]
"Because you Christians think homosexuality is wrong."

---

10. Other sins are listed in this passage, but I isolated the sexual sins since that is my focus here.

"Well, to be more precise, it's the behavior that's the problem. But do you think Christians think *all* sex outside of marriage is wrong?"

"Yes."

"So, do you think God hates heterosexuals, too?"

"Maybe."

"God doesn't hate gays. He hates sin. It doesn't matter what kind it is. That means every single one of us is in trouble—me, too. We all need forgiveness—gays and non-gays alike."

5. Here's another:

"The Bible doesn't condemn loving, consensual, same-sex relationships—only exploitive, abusive, and oppressive ones."

"Do you feel the same about adultery?"

"Of course not!"

"Why not?"

"The Bible clearly says adultery is wrong."

"What if the adulterers have a loving, consensual relationship?"

"It's still wrong."

"So, Scripture condemns the act of adultery, even if it's a loving relationship?"

"That's right."

"Have you read what Romans 1 says about homosexuality?"

"Sure."

"Does it condemn the act itself, like the passages that condemn adultery?"

"Yes, but Paul was only condemning abusive gay relationships, not loving ones."

"Where does it say that in the passage?"

"We know that in Paul's culture, those relationships were abusive."

"But I'm not talking about the culture. I'm talking about the Bible verse. Does Paul make any reference to abusive relationships or make any exception for loving relationships?"

6. Here's a final short one:

> "What's wrong with love? Love is love. Why is God against two people loving each other?"
>
> "Why would you think God is against love?"
>
> "Because you think loving, gay relationships are wrong."
>
> "Is sex the same as love?"
>
> "Well, no."
>
> "God agrees with you. They're not the same. He wants us to love one another. That's for everybody. God reserves sex, though, for the kind of relationship he created it for—heterosexual marriage."

VI. What Main Points Did We Cover in This Session?

A. First, I addressed the "Silent Christ" maneuver.
1. Even if Jesus was silent on certain issues, his silence doesn't imply his approval.
2. You can't conclude anything about what Jesus *approved* of based on what he *did not condemn*.
3. As far as we know, Jesus didn't say anything about slavery, capital punishment, spousal abuse, sex trafficking, racism, or child sacrifice.

B. Second, we looked at God's purpose from the beginning for sex and marriage.
1. Jesus answered a challenge regarding marriage by going back to the creation order at the very beginning.
2. There are three critical takeaways from his teaching:
    a. First, Jesus affirmed the commonsense observation that human gender is binary.
    b. Second, marriage is between a man and a woman, a biological male and a female.
    c. Third, the only kind of sexuality that is proper in Jesus' view is sex between a man and a woman who are committed to each other for life in marriage.

C. **Next, we talked about why pronouns matter and how to navigate those challenging waters.**
   1. In our culture, we're pressured to reject both God's truth and common sense to affirm a false narrative of reality.
   2. Our general approach is to respond as Jesus did.
      a. We protect people's feelings (show grace)—within reason . . .
      b. But we reject the narrative (uphold truth).
   3. Three separate circumstances require three different responses.
      a. First, call people by the names they choose for themselves.
      b. Second, if you're required to post your "preferred" pronoun, don't simply report your accurate biological gender. Identify your biological sex, instead.
      c. Third, if you're asked to use preferred pronouns when speaking of others, then graciously—but firmly—refuse.

D. **Finally, I addressed the question of the Bible and sex, especially the issue of homosexuality and Scripture.**
   1. According to Jesus, the only kind of sex honoring to God is intimacy between a man and a woman in the lifelong committed relationship of marriage.
   2. Any sex outside of heterosexual marriage is a corruption of God's good design and inconsistent with being a member of God's kingdom. This includes homosexuality.
      a. God designed men and women to *function* sexually together. Their bodies fit together in a precise way to make sexual union possible.
      b. Homosexuality is a rejection of the appropriate sexual counterpart God has provided—a woman who was built by God to be man's sexual complement.
   3. The "not that kind of homosexuality" argument fails.
      a. Claim: Scripture only prohibits same-sex behavior that was exploitive, abusive, and oppressive instead of loving, caring, and committed.
      b. However, when it comes to sex, Scripture condemns the *behavior*, not the *relationship*.
         (1) There is not the slightest hint in any passage that same-sex activity is only a problem when it is coercive or oppressive.

(2) This principle applies exactly the same way to all sinful sexual activity, including adultery and fornication.

4. God's solution for satisfying our sexual appetites is lifelong heterosexual marriage.

[?] Self-Assessment

Try to answer the following questions without using your notes.

1. Describe the "Silent Christ" maneuver.
    ▸ People employ "Silent Christ" when they claim that because Jesus never _____ or _____ certain behaviors, then Jesus must have _____ of them.

2. What is the problem with "Silent Christ"?
    ▸ You can't conclude anything about what Jesus _____ of based on what he did not _____.

3. What was the key move Jesus made to answer questions about marriage and divorce?
    ▸ Jesus answered the question about marriage by going back to the very _____, to the _____ order.

4. What are the three crucial takeaways from Jesus' comments?
    ▸ First, Jesus affirmed the commonsense observation that human gender is _____. Second, marriage is between a _____ and a _____, a biological _____ and a _____. Third, the only kind of sex that is proper is sex between a _____ and a _____ who are _____ to each other for life in _____.

5. Why are pronouns not inconsequential?
    ▸ Because with pronouns we are pressured to reject both God's _____ and common _____ to affirm a _____ narrative of reality.

6. What are the responses to the three separate circumstances you'll face with pronoun use?

▸ First, call people by the _____ they choose for themselves. Second, if required to post "preferred" pronouns, don't simply report your accurate biological _____. Identify your biological _____ instead. Third, if asked to use preferred pronouns when speaking of others, then graciously—but firmly—_____.

7. In a single sentence, sum up Jesus' view of marriage.
   ▸ According to Jesus, marriage is one _____ with _____ woman, becoming one _____ for one _____.

8. What is the "not that kind of homosexuality" argument (aka the "cultural distance" argument)?
   ▸ According to this claim, Scripture *only* prohibits same-sex behavior that is _____, abusive, and _____ instead of loving, _____, and _____.

9. Simply put, why, according to Scripture, does the argument fail?
   ▸ When it comes to sex, Scripture condemns the _____, not the _____.

✓ Self-Assessment with Answers

1. People employ "Silent Christ" when they claim that because Jesus never **mentioned** or **condemned** certain behaviors, then Jesus must have **approved** of them.
2. You can't conclude anything about what Jesus **approved** of based on what he did not **condemn**.
3. Jesus answered the question about marriage by going back to the very **beginning**, to the **creation** order.
4. First, Jesus affirmed the commonsense observation that human gender is **binary**. Second, marriage is between a **man** and a **woman**, a biological **male** and a **female**. Third, the only kind of sex that is proper is sex between a **man** and a **woman** who are **committed** to each other for life in **marriage**.
5. Because with pronouns we are pressured to reject both God's **truth** and common **sense** to affirm a **false** narrative of reality.
6. First, call people by the **names** they choose for themselves. Second, if required to post "preferred" pronouns, don't simply report your accurate biological **gender**.

Identify your biological **sex** instead. Third, if asked to use preferred pronouns when speaking of others, then graciously—but firmly—**refuse**.

7. According to Jesus, marriage is one **man** with **one** woman, becoming one **flesh** for one **lifetime**.

8. According to this claim, Scripture *only* prohibits same-sex behavior that is **exploitive**, abusive, and **oppressive** instead of loving, **caring**, and **committed**.

9. When it comes to sex, Scripture condemns the **behavior**, not the **relationship**.

Interactive Group Study Questions

1. Discuss how many who identify as Christian embrace ideas that are completely at odds with the Bible—especially when it comes to sex. Why do you think this is happening?
2. What is the "Silent Christ" objection? What is its *apparent* strength, and what are its serious weaknesses?
3. Explain the three crucial takeaways from Jesus' teaching on divorce. How do these principles give us insight into Jesus' opinion on sex, gender, and marriage?
4. What statement has Greg found to be the best way to sum up Jesus' view of marriage? How does this simple summary address multiple issues in a single sentence?
5. Discuss why pronouns are important. How has the pronoun issue become the skirmish line in a battle of worldviews?
6. Talk about ways we can resist the lies, live the truth, and still be kind.
7. How would you answer someone who claims that the same-sex behavior condemned in the Bible is not what modern-day LGBT Christians practice?

Going Deeper: Information for Self-Study

Explain to a friend the things you've covered in this lesson.

1. Explain to him the problems with the "Silent Christ" approach to assessing the morality of controversial behaviors.
2. Describe the general strategy Jesus used when answering questions about marriage and what the implications are for our current discussions.

3. Share with your friend the three different challenges facing us with pronouns and how to respond to them.
4. Sum up for him in a single sentence what Jesus' view of marriage was and the broader conclusions we can draw from it.
5. Describe the "not that kind of homosexuality" attempt to deflect scriptural prohibitions of gay sex and explain what's wrong with that approach.
6. Be prepared to share your experiences with the group when you get together next time.

 Food for Thought

"Sex" versus "Gender"

At the moment, the claim that gender is binary and connected with one's physical sex is controversial. Some think there's no vital connection between a person's physical sex and their mental perception of their sex (often referred to as "gender" or "gender identity"). And, indeed, there is a minuscule percentage of people who are genuinely conflicted, thinking their own gender is different from their sex. But that is not the way it was in the beginning.

This internal conflict is known as "gender dysphoria." The apparent explosion of gender dysphoria (called "rapid onset" gender dysphoria) is clearly a recent phenomenon and suggests that cultural pressure—what some have called a "social contagion"—is the principle driving force. In simple terms, transgenderism is a fad, though a profoundly destructive one.[11]

For the Children

It's easy to resist any suggestion that marriage and family are fundamentally connected to children. Clearly, not all families have kids. Some marriages are barren by choice or by circumstance. This proves nothing, though.

The natural marriage/procreation connection is not nullified because in some cases children are not intended or even possible. The state protects conjugal marriage because

---

11. See Abigail Shrier, *Irreversible Damage: The Transgender Craze Seducing Our Daughters* (Washington, DC: Regnery, 2020). See also Nancy Pearcey, *Love Thy Body: Answering Hard Questions about Love and Sexuality* (Grand Rapids: Baker, 2018).

of its institutional importance to culture. Pointing out exceptional cases doesn't nullify the general rule.

The fact that same-sex couples can legally adopt changes nothing. This, too, subverts the purpose of marriage by robbing children of a vital ingredient: mothers and fathers. By licensing same-sex marriage, society declares by law that two men or two women are equally suited to raise a child, that mothers and fathers contribute nothing unique to healthy child-rearing. This is self-evidently false. Moms and dads are not interchangeable.

EPILOGUE

That's *Street Smarts*—maneuvering in tough conversations, using a plan with specific questions meant to expose a weakness or a flaw in someone's view. It's easier than you think if you follow the steps.

First, get a clear take on your friend's view. Make sure you understand it. If there are any ambiguities, clarify with your first Columbo question, "What do you mean by that?" (or some variation).

Second, reflect on the challenge or do some research to zero in on its weaknesses or failings. I've provided material here in *Street Smarts* to help you see flaws in popular challenges to Christianity, but many other sources are available to help you.[1]

Third, chart a course for your conversation—as I have done for you in the examples in this study guide—using a mixture of questions (especially clarification questions) to keep your friend engaged while you move forward to expose the liabilities you've discovered. Try to have the first couple of moves clear in your mind—even memorized—so that when the challenge comes up, you'll have your first questions at the ready. This single bit of prep will save you lots of stress.

You may need to plan ahead and practice a bit, doing conversation "dry runs." As you put these principles into practice, though, the process will become almost second nature—a kind of mental "muscle memory." You'll be able to move ahead easily in conversations

---

1. My book *Tactics* can also be a benefit by providing a series of maneuvers—with plenty of anecdotes and illustrations—to help you be more effective on the street.

that used to be daunting and discomfiting, staying securely in the driver's seat on a productive route.

Finally, **trust God.** No matter how clever you sound, everything you say will turn to dust if God's Spirit is not in it. No matter how poorly you think you've acquitted yourself, even the most meager effort can turn to gold if God decides to move. Never presume on God either way. Be faithful in the moment, then let God do his part—which is all the rest. You don't need to "tune in" to the Spirit. Encounters on the street don't usually work that way. Rather, simply do what you can, then trust in God's sovereign control.

Be brave, trust God, step out, and give 'em heaven.

www.ingramcontent.com/pod-product-compliance
Lightning Source LLC
Chambersburg PA
CBHW080351170426
43194CB00014B/2754